OVERTHINKING

A Complete Guide on How to Stop Worrying, Reduce Your Anxiety, Eliminate Negative Thinking, Declutter Your Mind and Focus on the Present

By

Robert Handler

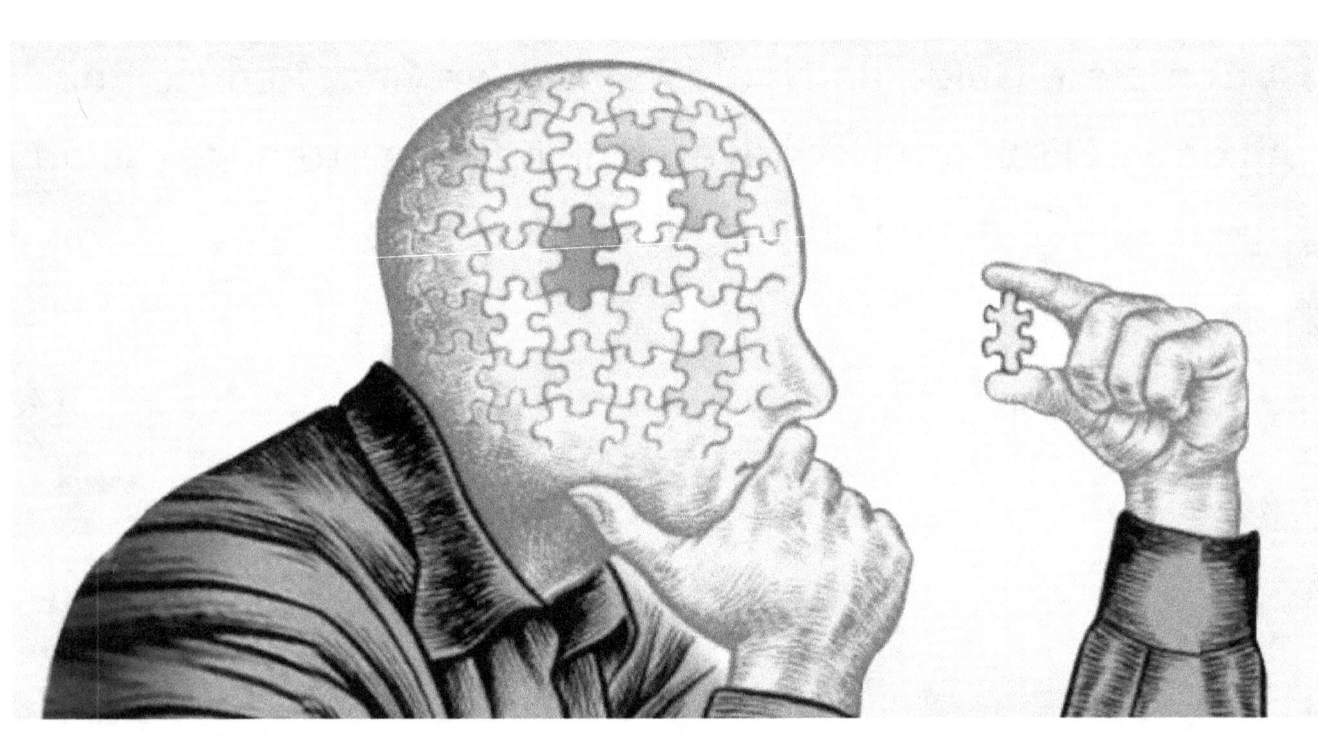

© Copyright 2021 - All rights reserved.

The following Book is reproduced below with the goal of providing information that is as accurate and reliable as possible. Regardless, purchasing this Book can be seen as consent to the fact that both the publisher and the author of this book are in no way experts on the topics discussed within and that any recommendations or suggestions that are made herein are for entertainment purposes only. Professionals should be consulted as needed prior to undertaking any of the action endorsed herein.

This declaration is deemed fair and valid by both the American Bar Association and the Committee of Publishers Association and is legally binding throughout the United States.

Furthermore, the transmission, duplication, or reproduction of any of the following work including specific information will be considered an illegal act irrespective of if it is done electronically or in print. This extends to creating a secondary or tertiary copy of the work or a recorded copy and is only allowed with the express written consent from the Publisher. All additional right reserved.

The information in the following pages is broadly considered a truthful and accurate account of facts and as such, any inattention, use, or misuse of the information in question by the reader will render any resulting actions solely under their purview. There are no scenarios in which the publisher or the original author of this work can be in any fashion deemed liable for any hardship or damages that may befall them after undertaking information described herein.

Additionally, the information in the following pages is intended only for informational purposes and should thus be thought of as universal. As befitting its nature, it is presented without assurance regarding its prolonged validity or interim quality. Trademarks that are mentioned are done without written consent and can in no way be considered an endorsement from the trademark holder.

Table of Contents

Introduction

It is effortless to fall into the device of overthinking about minor things throughout everyday life. So, when you are contemplating something, pose necessary inquiries to yourself. It has been found through an exploration that extending the viewpoint by utilizing these straightforward inquiries can snap you rapidly out of overthinking.

Endeavor to set brief time-limits for choices. So, figure out how to turn out to be better at settling on opportunities and to get a move on setting due dates in your everyday life. Regardless of when it is a little or a more excellent choice.

Be a person of movement. When you understand how in the first place making a move dependably, then you will wait less by overthinking. Setting due dates is one thing that will assist you with being a person of activity.

State stop in a condition where you understand you can't think straight. Now and again, when you are avaricious or when you are lying in bed and are going to rest, by the negative thoughts start murmuring around in your mind.

Do whatever it takes not to wind up stirred up in vague feelings of trepidation. Another snare that you have fallen into ordinarily that have impelled on overthinking is that you have lost all sense of direction in dubious feelings of fear about a circumstance in your life. Thus, your mind running wild has made fiasco situations about what could occur if you accomplish something. What is the most terrible that could happen? You ought to figure out how to pose this inquiry to yourself.

Invest the vast majority of your energy right now. Be right now in your regular day to day existence instead of before or a conceivable future. Hinder how you do whatever you are doing well at this point. Move slower, talk slower, or ride your bike all the more gradually, for instance. By doing as such, you become increasingly mindful of how you utilize your body and what's going on surrounding you at present.

Endeavor to invest the more significant part of your energy with individuals who don't think more. Your social condition has considerable influence. Discover approaches to spend the more substantial portion of your energy and consideration with the general population and sources that effects affect your reasoning.

Countering Overthinking: Step Towards an Improved Life

So, suppose you're hanging about at a social event, encompassed by partners and customers, and you have spotted somebody you genuinely need to converse with. Perhaps it is business related, or you need to develop personal ties. How it is, you set up a psychological draft of what to state, as one does and means to meet them however a shivering apprehension in the back of your head leaves you speechless. Consider the possibility that they would prefer not to chat with you. Imagine a scenario where the specific line of discussion doesn't work out. Or then again even turns out badly? Your dread makes a kind of domino impact, and you start to think about the most terrible that could occur as the inescapable. With each idea, you are maneuvered further into the tangled wreckage of perplexity inside your psyche, and this, eventually, renders you unfit to try and talk any longer. You at that point, watch as someone else engages in discussion with the subject: an open door lost.

Overthinking and the resulting fretfulness and tension, while demonstrates to be a considerable hindrance in one's social and personal life, is additionally shockingly normal and for each person who is an injured individual to it, turns into the reason for circumstances lost and minutes that one would later lament. In any case, with a couple of day by day rehearses and a decoded frame of mind, it tends to be defeated effectively.

Acknowledgment

The initial move towards managing intemperate overthinking and tension is tolerating the issue in any case. Directly after this, would you have the option to feel free to settle it? In any case, while realizing that you are a remunerator is significant, it is likewise indispensable that you understand that you are not the only one in the circumstance and that there is no motivation to freeze. Overthinking is a common thing among many individuals today, and you would almost certainly beat it with an inspirational demeanor.

The best minute is the present minute.

One good precedent is relaxing. You'd be shocked at how much this makes a difference. Close your eyes and take full breaths for several minutes. Intently watching and taking full breaths help to pull you in the present minute and helps in clearing your head.

Another good precedent is reflecting on rehearsing care. The essential thought is to stay quiet and just spotlight on all that is around you intently, and this has done some incredible things for many individuals. Just once every day, close your eyes and attempt to take in the entirety of your environment. Tune in to your considerations; however, don't 'connect' with them, and inevitably, you can try to cut back their 'volume.'

Notwithstanding that, back off. Do all that you do with full consciousness of you doing it. Attempt and describe to yourself each progression that you make, and power yourself to see your environment. This will likewise assist you with staying right now.

Be certain

At the point when full to the overflow with confidence and liking yourself, you develop a positive outlook. You would end up to be less inclined to overthinking; thus, everything that you do or say ends up being improved. The first things you can do is get occupied. Structure an arrangement of what to accomplish for the afternoon and continue being profitable. Doing things shield your brain from straying, and notwithstanding that, completing stuff results in an extraordinary lift in certainty through a feeling of achievement. You ought to likewise attempt and accomplish something you're great at any rate once every day. Regardless of whether you're a specialist at playing an instrument or you have a remarkable ability for a computer game, take a break from your calendar and do it. It'll be an incredible assistance.

Another life-changing change you can make is to counterfeit it. This may sound hard, yet this works extraordinary. Imagine that you're a character you know, who is smart, intelligent, and sure about themselves. Maybe you know one from a TV program, a motion picture or a book. Feel free to convey all that you state with certainty, regardless of whether you don't know of it, or you're panicked. You'll see that as you counterfeit it to an ever-increasing extent, in the end, you acquire that trust, in actuality.

Give up

Endeavoring to control every one of incredible results is, without a doubt, the fundamental driver for compensation. Since when you do, you are likewise destined to hotly consider what to do in each snapshot of your life in dread of what could like this occur straightaway. The best thing you can do is to persuade yourself not to. Understand that you have nothing to do with what happens in your life, and thus, there is no motivation to stress over it. The universe has your destiny chosen, so you should make the most out of each minute. Attempt and understand this before anything you may falter do, and it'll assist you with stopping overthinking and take care of business.

Something else you can do make explicit time allotments to settle on any choice. Regardless of whether it is to proceed to converse with somebody or more significant life decisions which may constrain you to overthink. Pause for a moment for the little ones and a couple of days for the bigger ones in life and no more. This would push you to survey a choice usually and research to settle on the ideal decision. When you do decide on an opportunity, steel yourself and do what needs to be done. It may scare yet you'll see it remunerating toward the end.

By the day's end, the most significant piece to acknowledge is that we as a whole hold the possibility to accomplish all that we have longed for, and the main thing we need to do is to steel ourselves and evacuate our hindrances. What's more, that has a significant effect.

After all the diligent work, this ought to be the season when we at long last quit worrying and begin having fun. How would you stop those annoying 'imagine a scenario where?' stresses are swarming back.

We as a whole do it once in a while - stress over things we've said or done, examine disposable remarks others have or invest hours dismembering the significance of a specific email or letter. Nearly without acknowledging it, we get sucked into a winding of negative contemplations and feelings that take our delight and excitement. It's an example that a few clinicians bring over reasoning. The underlying considerations lead to progressively negative musings, the inquiries to more inquiries. The over reasoning turns into a course that matures and fabricates so that everything gains out of power. Stall out in this negative cycle, and it can influence your life. It can likewise prompt some downright awful choices when generally little issues turn out to be so dramatically overemphasized that you lose your point of view on them.

When we over think-focusing on what has occurred previously (future) - we are obliterating the minute we are in. You pass up encountering and appreciating the present time and place of your life.

For what reason do we do it? - At the most fundamental dimension, the science of our cerebrum makes it simple to overthink. Musings and recollections don't merely sit in our cerebrums segregated and free from one another - they are woven together in mind-boggling systems of affiliations. One consequence of all these perplexing interconnections is that musings concerning a specific issue in your life can trigger considerations about other associated problems.

A large portion of us has some negative recollections, stresses over the future, or worries about the present. A significant part of the time we're most likely not aware of these negative musings. In any case, when they come over us, regardless of whether it's because the climate's terrible or because we alcoholic an excessive amount of wine, it's simpler to review the negative recollections and start the cycle of over reasoning. Numerous ladies are over-burden with juggling home and work responsibilities and want to do everything superbly. We will, in general feel in charge of everybody, a figure we ought to be in charge and set ourselves strangely particular requirements.

How to defeat it? - If you're endless over scholar, just being advised to invest significant time and unwind won't do it for you. You have to find a way to control and conquer contrary reasoning. Ending the propensity isn't simple, and there's no enchantment answer for everybody, except these are a portion of the means that specialists propose can enable you to break out of the negative cycle of over reasoning.

1. Offer yourself a reprieve - Free your brain with something that draws in your fixation and lifts your mindset - regardless of whether it's perusing a decent book, strolling the canine, having a back rub or doing the rec center.

2. Take yourself close by - When you see yourself going over similar musings, let yourself know immovably to stop — post yellow stickers around your work area and the house as updates.

3. Jettison the postponing strategies - If there are specific circumstances or spots that trigger over reasoning, for example, a work area heaped high with papers or open letters or messages, at that point take care of business, anyway little. Over reasoning that is connected with inertia can turn into an endless

loop. Rather than living in dread of what you can't do and what could occur, it's far superior to handle it virtually by accomplishing something.

4. Discharge your contemplations - Issues that expect large extents after frantic stressing can all of a sudden dissolve away when you talk them through with a companion. They can appear to be absurd or even amusing. Making a joke out of them can genuinely defuse your stresses.

5. Plan for deduction time - choose when you enable yourself to think. Point of confinement the time you give yourself and adhere to your timetable. Envision keeping every one of those contemplations in a single box that you can take out at a specific time, at that point seal and put it away when the time runs out.

6. Appreciate the occasion - Actively plan things that you understand. It doesn't make a difference what it is - whatever works for you. It's difficult to grieve in negative over reasoning when you're having some good times.

7. Express your feelings - Instead of going into a profound examination of what your feelings truly mean, enable yourself to encounter them for a change. Sob, shout, punch a pad, will allow yourself to feel the warmth and after that proceed onward.

8. Pardon yourself - That doesn't mean imagining that slight or harmful comments never occurred, yet it means settling on a decision to set them aside as opposed to harp on them.

9. Be careful - Take time every day to be at the time. It won't be simple, however, persevere, and you'll receive the benefits. Go out in the greenhouse to watch the dusk, go through 15 minutes in the recreation center at noon or sit in a bistro all alone. Try not to exile the considerations, let them travel every which way, yet see what's near and how your body feels

Chapter 1.   What is Overthinking?

There are many ways of describing overthinking. It can be understood as a situation where one cannot stop worrying and thinking about things. Overthinking is not a disorder. It involves a fear that grows in you and overwhelms you, but you can't help yourself but let it do so. In some cases, instead of crying it out, you simply opt to hold back your tears. It's the fear of failure: failing at your job, failing a certain class, failing in your relationships. Overthinking drives you to work hard for unrealistic expectations. This might sound productive, but in reality, you will be exhausted by maintaining this pace. Thinking too much leads to exhaustion. Emotionally and physically, you will feel exhausted since your mind never stops. It is always flooded with thoughts and the worst thing about it is that you believe there is nothing you can do.

Overthinking is that inner voice that tries to bring you down. It criticizes you and destroys your confidence and self-esteem. You not only doubt yourself, but you also doubt those who are close to you. It pushes you to second guess everything. Thinking too much can be compared to a spreading fire. It burns down everything that it finds on its way. Therefore, you will suffer as a result of overthinking.

Overthinking is when your mind clings to the faults that you have made and takes you through them throughout the day. When you overthink, your life will be on constant pause. You will always feel as though you are waiting for the right moment to do something. The problem is that this moment never arrives. You're always anticipating that something could go wrong. You will be overly careful when doing anything. This is influenced by the fact that you are just worried things might not work out as expected.

The following are clear indications that you think too much. You might try to deny it, but consider these signs and question yourself whether these are some of the things that you might have experienced.

You Overanalyze Everything

If you notice that you overanalyze everything around you, then you are certainly an overthinker. This means that you may try to find a deeper meaning in all the experiences that you go through. When meeting new people, instead of engaging in productive communication, you may focus instead on how other people perceive you. Someone could be giving you a particular look and you may make several assumptions just based on that look. Overthinking consumes you. You end up wasting a lot of energy trying to figure out and make sense of the world around you. What you don't realize is that not everything has intrinsic meaning.

You Think Too Much, But Don't Act

An overthinker will be affected by something called analysis paralysis. This is a scenario where you think too much about something, but don't do anything about it in the end. In this case, you spend a lot of time weighing the options you have at your disposal. At first, you make up your mind on what the best alternative might be. Later, you compare your decision to other possible decisions that you could take. This means that you can't stop thinking about the possibilities and whether or not you made the right decision. Ultimately, you end up not making a decision. You only find yourself in a vicious circle where you simply think a lot, but there is little that you do. Perhaps the best strategy to prevent yourself from falling into a thinking trap is to try out the alternatives you have. A simple decision to act will make a huge difference.

You Can't Let Go

Often, we make erroneous decisions that could lead us to fail. When this happens, it can be daunting to let go more so when you reflect on the sacrifices you have made to get to the point you are at. You might feel that it is painful to let go after you have invested a lot of money on a certain business. The issue here is that you don't want to fail. However, it is important to realize that failing to let go only holds you back from trying out something else that could work. It also affects your life since you will think repeatedly about your failures. You need to move on. It's important that you shift your attention to something else instead of beating yourself up over something that is now out of your control. Convince yourself that there is nothing you can do about what has already happened apart from learning from it. The best thing you can do is to let go and move on.

You Always Want to Know Why
Without a doubt, the notion of asking why can be helpful to solve problems. This is because this probing attitude gets you the answers that you might be looking for. Nonetheless, it can also be damaging when you can't help but always wonder why. Normally, we are accustomed to answering questions from kids. They just love to ask why about anything and everything. They will not hesitate to ask you why you don't talk to your neighbor. Why children are born or simply why you love to walk. There's something unique about how children are curious. Overthinkers maintain such investigative attitude throughout their lives. As adults, there are certain things that only have surface meanings. Therefore, probing too much can only affect how other people see you.

You Analyze People
The way you see other people can also say a lot about you. In most cases, you get lost thinking too much about how other people behave. You may tend to judge everybody that you come across. This one walks in a funny way. That

person is not dressed well. You wonder what someone sitting at the park is smiling about. When these thoughts fill your head, you will only drain yourself. Spending too much time focusing on other people will only deter you from using your mind productively. Instead of visualizing your goals and your future, you waste your energy mulling over little things that add no value to you.

Regular Insomnia

Do you find it hard to sleep sometimes? You may get worked up over the idea that your brain cannot shut down and stop thinking. Sadly, this can paralyze you since your brain doesn't get the rest that it deserves. Gradually, you will notice a decrease in your productivity. You are unlikely to feel good about yourself since there is little that you achieve. Worrying too much about not being able to sleep can make you uneasy and you may find yourself in a state of captivity. If this is something that you have been experiencing, then it sounds like you might be an overthinker. What could you do about this? First, if you are not active, then it is vital that you find a way of keeping yourself busy. In addition, meditation is a great practice that can help you stop overthinking and relax and focus on the present.

You Always Live in Fear

Are you afraid about what the future has in store for you? If you answer yes to this question, then chances are that you're caged in your mind. Living in fear could drive you to resort to drugs and alcohol as your best remedy.

You will gain the perception that by taking drugs, it will help you drown your sorrows and help you forget. Unfortunately, this is not the case since drugs and alcohol are mere depressants. They slow down your brain functioning. As a result, you tend to believe that they are helping you forget.

You're Always Fatigued

Do you always wake up in the morning feeling tired? This could be a result of stress or depression. Instead of living a productive life, you find yourself waking up late, tired, and unmotivated. The reason why this happens is because you don't give your mind an opportunity to rest. It has been working day and night. In the evening, instead of sleeping you find yourself awake all night because you are overthinking. Your mind cannot work for 24 hours straight at the same level of functioning. You will only suffer from burnouts. You need to give your mind ample time to rest and reboot.

You Don't Live in the Present

Do you find it difficult to enjoy life? Why do you think you find it daunting to sit back, relax, and be happy with your friends? The mere fact that you can't stay in the present implies that you won't focus on what is happening in the present. Overthinking will blind you from noticing anything good that is currently happening around you. You will often think about the worst that can happen. The issue is that you are trapped in your mind and there is nothing outside your thoughts that you can constructively think about.

Failure to live in the present denies you the opportunity to improve relationships with other people. In fact, you will live in fear that they will criticize you. Therefore, you will only want to exist in your cocoon. Again, this will lead to stress.

Types of Overthinking

There are different forms of overthinking that could affect the quality of the decisions we make. Common forms of overthinking are succinctly discussed in the following paragraphs.

Abstract Thinking

This refers to a form of thinking which goes beyond concrete realities. For instance, when you are trying to formulate theories to explain your observations, then you're engaging in abstract thinking. When your business is not performing well, you might jump to the conclusion that it's because of the economy.

Complexity

The complexity form of overthinking comes about when there are many factors to consider in your decision-making process. In this case, these numerous factors could prevent you from weighing the true importance of each one of them. The effect is that it could prevent you from making decisions promptly.

Avoidance

Avoidance occurs when one tries to avoid doing something by using the decision-making process as their excuse.

Cold Logic

When using cold logic to think, you tend to avoid relying on human factors, including language, culture, personality, emotion, and social dynamics. The outcome is that you end up making biased decisions that do not consider legal or social realities.

Intuition Neglect

This occurs when one fails to consider what they already know. In other words, one opts to overthink something that they already know a thing or two about.

Instead of following your gut instinct, you overthink and end up making the wrong decisions.

Creating Problems

You may also find yourself thinking in a way where you are creating problems that are not there in the first place. There are certain situations or things which are not as complex as you think. In ordinary situations, it would have taken you a minute or two to solve them. It is vital to focus more on the bigger picture and not nitpick at the details. Sometimes it is important to see things as they are. Don't complicate your life by thinking of potential problems.

Magnifying the Issue

Usually, small problems require simple solutions. There are instances where we amplify these problems and we end up coming up with overly complex solutions to solve them. This is another form of overthinking. You end up wasting your resources to come up with huge solutions that don't match the problems you are experiencing.

Fear of Failure

Fear of failure is not a new concept to most people. In fact, this is what motivates most of us to work hard. Instead of working hard for a bright future, you find yourself drawing motivation from the fear you have developed inside you.

Irrelevant Decisions

There are times when we make irrelevant decisions because we force ourselves to make these decisions, yet we are not required to make them. For instance, when thinking about our future, there are instances where we end up making irrelevant decisions based on assumptions.

Getting married, for example, based on the assumptions you have, you might conclude that you need to get married because you're getting old.

Causes of Overthinking

After looking at the possible signs that could indicate you are an overthinker and the types of overthinking, it is important to reflect on the causes. While reading through this section, ask yourself: what causes you to overthink? Frankly, depending on the situation that you might be going through, there are varying reasons why you may think too much. For instance, your fear of embarrassment could push you to overthink what you should wear or how you should present yourself in front of other people. On the other hand, the fear of failure can lead you to work hard towards achieving your goals.

The following are common reasons why you may overthink.

Lack of Confidence

Lack of confidence is one of the main reasons why people tend to overthink. When you're not sure about what to do, it opens doors for uncertainty. Your mind is filled with fear as a result. It is worth noting that you can never be sure about the decisions that you make. Accordingly, there are times when you will be required to take risks when making important decisions. Taking such risks prevents you from torturing your mind since you will be acting without spending too much time thinking. Deciding to do something gives you confidence. This will have an impact on how you handle problems in your life. With time, you will develop into more of a decision maker than a thinker.

Second-Guessing Yourself

Still on the issue of confidence, doubting yourself is mentally exhausting. Sure, it is understandable that you may make the wrong decisions. No one is perfect, so don't expect that you will always make the right choices. However, constantly being indecisive will rob you of your confidence. The main issue here is that you will frequently stress yourself over anything that requires you to make a choice.

To avoid second-guessing yourself, it is crucial that you trust your abilities. This will be helpful as you will become more self-aware and in turn, end up making sound decisions. The exciting thing is that you will avoid the notion of repeatedly asking other people for their opinions before doing anything.

Being a Constant Worrier

Research shows that severe anxiety is a widespread issue among American teenagers. Most of them are afraid that they might fail in their lives. In addition, they always worry too much about the world around them. As a result, it is not surprising that they tend to worry about what others think about them. The habit of constantly worrying that things could go wrong will push you to overthink. The images that you develop in your mind will mostly feature the thoughts of failing. Frankly, this drains energy from you.

Instead of worrying too much about the future, you should understand that thinking positively and constructively about how to accomplish your goals is more productive. Remember, the future is uncertain to everybody. No one knows what will happen tomorrow. Therefore, the best thing that you can do about the future is to plan for it. Changing your mentality to focus more on the goals you have set and how you can achieve them will motivate you to live a life with a sense of direction. The best part is that the sense of optimism you develop will help you see life from a positive perspective.

Overthinking Acts as Protection

You might find yourself thinking too much because it is a way of safeguarding yourself from your life's troubles. The reality is that you are afraid to take action. Therefore, overthinking only thwarts your progress in life. You will only be held captive by your thoughts. It is worth realizing that it is beneficial to act even when you're not sure about yourself.

Consider the benefits you gain from the experiences you face in your life. These experiences make you stronger. You will be more aware of the pros and cons of engaging in certain activities since you have experienced them. Avoid falling for the idea that overthinking will protect you from your problems. It's better to face your challenges head-on.

You Cannot Relax

It will be difficult for your mind to stop thinking if you pay too much attention to the problem that you are facing. Your problems will put you in a state of constant tension. The worst thing is that you haven't invested your time in learning how to relax. For that reason, it will be difficult to eliminate negative thoughts from your mind. Individuals who value the importance of working out or meditating and engaging in yoga exercises can prevent their minds from overthinking. Meditation works to help you connect your mind and body.

Therefore, through this self-awareness, you can identify the existence of negative thoughts and learn how to separate yourself from them.

You Yearn for Perfection

Being a perfectionist might be perceived as a good thing at first. However, there is a huge price to pay to live as a perfectionist. Often, you will want everything to fall into place just like you want it. You will never be satisfied with anything that comes up short of what you had anticipated. Therefore, this means that you will always overthink about what needs to be done. Your mind will be in a constant loop of overthinking things, whether they are done in the right way or not. Developing such a habit will only cause detrimental effects to both your mental and physical health.

Chapter 2.   Declutter Your Mind

We live in a world that requires us to act on many things. Besides overcoming daily stressors, we should learn how to develop the right habits that prevent us from worrying and thinking negative thoughts. The strenuous environment and the hustle and bustle we have to face often fills our minds with clutter. It often reaches a point where our minds can't stop thinking. You may become overwhelmed with thoughts which leaves your mind in a total mess. Does this sound like you? If yes, then your mind is waving a white flag at you and may require some decluttering.

In the same way that you will regularly spare some time to declutter your office and your house, the mind also requires decluttering. This will guarantee that you free up some space for optimal functioning. However, it is not as easy as it sounds since you cannot see exactly what is in the mind. As a result, the cleaning process will be different from the normal decluttering that you have been used to. So, how do you empty out the unnecessary from your mind? This chapter will focus on answering this question and it will help you understand the significance of decluttering your mind.

Causes of Mental Clutter

In an ordinary case, when cleaning your home or office, you will start by identifying the items that are causing clutter. Likewise, before decluttering your mind, it is important that you start by identifying the causes of mental clutter. The importance of doing this is that it guarantees that you can effectively deal with clutter in the long run. You will be more aware of the factors that contribute to clutter in your mind and work to avoid them.

The following are some of the common causes of mental clutter.

Overwhelm

Naturally, if you are overwhelmed with things, then it will lead to disorder in your mind. As a result, it will be daunting for you to establish a reasonable way of dealing with your issues. This causes clutter. Fortunately, you can overcome this by acknowledging the fact that you can't handle everything at once. This means that you should break down your tasks into smaller, yet manageable mini-tasks. Handle these things one at a time. At the end of the day, you will realize that there is a lot that you have accomplished without feeling overwhelmed.

Over-Commitment

Committing yourself to finish certain activities on your to-do list is a good thing. Nonetheless, when you can't say no to other assignments, it means that you are over-committing yourself. Handling too many things will only lead to frustration. This is because there is a probability that you might fail to deliver. Learning to say no is an essential attribute of living a productive life. Saying no shouldn't be considered a bad thing since you're committing yourself to work productively on what you can manage. So, avoid over-committing yourself and taking on more than you can handle.

Fear

If you're afraid to let go of what has happened in the past, then are likely to strain your mind. The habit of holding on to things and thoughts often consumes us. Instead of working productively, your mind will keep ruminating on the past. This is pure clutter. Why should you put yourself through this torture when you can simply learn to let go?

Emotional Overload

Maybe your mind is filled with unwanted thoughts and feelings that keep draining energy from you. For instance, you might be dealing with a looming family crisis and it ends up affecting your productivity at work. If this is what you are going through, then it is best that you find time to deal with the issue. Ask for a leave of absence and free your mind from having to think over this matter repeatedly.

Lack of Time

Time will always be a prevalent issue. In everything that you do, you will often feel as though you don't have enough time. The reality is that there is enough time to handle all the important things in your life if you prioritize and plan effectively. Therefore, you shouldn't use the excuse that you lack time. The only issue here is that you may not know how to effectively manage your time. Organize yourself and prioritize what needs to be done first. This way, you will have more time to handle pending tasks on your to-do list.

Procrastination

If you are a victim of procrastination, then it comes as no surprise that your mind is always in a state of overdrive. Pushing things to be done at a later time means that there is a lot that will require your attention when 'later' comes. After a while, you will feel overwhelmed that you cannot complete everything on time. The problem began with the decision to procrastinate.

A Major Change in Life

Another reason why your mind might be filled with clutter is because of a major change which has occurred in your life. Frankly, sometimes we have to acknowledge the fact that change is inevitable. People fail to embrace change in their lives. As a result, they spend too much time doing what they used to do instead of changing. When faced with such predicaments, it is imperative that you evaluate what's going on in your life and strive to change.

Familiarity with the causes of mental clutter is the first step towards successful mental decluttering. Once you are aware of what causes clutter in your mind, you can develop practical solutions of how to get rid of them. It is worth bearing in mind that in most cases, there are multiple reasons why your mind is cluttered. So, open up your mind when trying to identify the factors that cause your messy mental state.

Practical Tips on How to Declutter Your Mind

Now that you understand what's causing all the clutter, let's look at some of the ways in which you can declutter your mind.

Set Priorities

Sometimes we fail to realize that a life without goals is a boring life. Living a goalless life is like wandering in the forest forever without a map. You don't have a particular destination that you want to reach. What's worse, you don't even know how to maneuver through the forest. Similarly, life without goals has no meaning. Your daily activities will be consumed with people and activities that don't add value to you. You will live in your comfort zone since there is nothing that you're actually targeting to achieve.

Setting priorities is a good place to start when looking to declutter your mind. This requires that you sit down and identify things that matter the most to your life. List down these goals and work to ensure that your actions are in line with the set goals. Setting priorities create structure with your to-do lists. You will begin to value the importance of delegating tasks when you feel like you can't handle them. More importantly, you will learn to say no since you comprehend the significance of handling only what you value and what you can take on.

Keep a Journal

Keeping a journal is a great strategy to help organize your thoughts. People tend to underestimate the power of noting down their thoughts every day. Journaling helps you rid your mind from things that you might not be aware of. It enhances your working memory and also guarantees that you can effectively manage stress. Similarly, the habit of noting down your daily experiences in a journal helps you express your emotions that may be bottled up within you. Therefore, you create space to experience new things in life. The effect of this is that you can relieve yourself from the anxiety that you might have been experiencing.

Learn to Let Go

Decluttering your mind can also be made easier if you learn to let go. Holding on to things in the past adds little or no value to your life. In fact, it only affects your emotional and mental wellbeing. The mere fact that you cannot let go implies that you will find it daunting to look ahead. Your mind will stagnate and this will stress you out. If you were a bird and you wanted to fly, what would you do? Without a doubt, you would want to free yourself from any burden that weighs you down. Apply this to real life and free yourself from any emotional baggage that you might be holding on to. Whether it's your failed past relationships or failed job opportunities, just let go. There is a greater reward in letting go since you open doors for new opportunities in your life.

Breathe

Breathing exercises would also be helpful in clearing clutter from your mind. There are certain forms of meditation that depend on breathing exercises to focus your attention on the breath. So, how do you practice breathing exercises? Start by taking a slow deep breath. Pause for a moment before exhaling. While breathing in and out, focus your mind on how you are breathing. Concentrate on how your breath goes in and out of your nose. It's relaxing, right? Practicing breathing exercises more often relaxes your mind. Besides helping you to relax, it boosts your immune system in profound ways. More about this will be discussed later in Chapter 6.

Declutter Your Physical Environment

If you live in a messy house, then there is a good chance that you're more likely frustrated. This may be because you find it difficult to find things you need. For instance, you end up wasting a lot of time looking for your car keys before heading to work. This affects how you start your day. You will be stressed that you arrived late and that there are numerous tasks waiting for you. Therefore, decluttering your physical space will also have a positive impact on your mind. Keeping things organized also means that your mind is virtually organized to handle the things that ought to be handled.

Learn to Share Your Thoughts

There is an overall positive feeling when you sit down to share your feelings with someone you care about. Instead of holding back your tears and emotions, sharing your feelings with your loved ones can clear emotional clutter from your mind. Have you ever wondered why you can think more clearly after sharing your sad feelings with another person? There is power in sharing your thoughts and feelings with other people. You can be more certain that you are making informed decisions since your mind can think clearly without being blinded by your emotions.

Curb Your Information Intake

The information that we consume affects the quality of the decisions we make. Unfortunately, the information we consume is sometimes unimportant to our lives. It only fills our minds with clutter and this prevents us from thinking clearly and making the right decisions. The worst thing is that it causes anxiety and stress as we tend to worry about the worst that could happen to us after what we have read or watched over the internet. Limiting what you consume from the internet can help prevent unwanted information from taking up space in your mind. So, instead of starting your day by checking your social media page, consider going for a walk or reading a book. The point here is that you should substitute your unproductive time on the internet by doing productive things.

Spare Some Time to Unwind

More importantly, to declutter your mind, you should consider taking a break. You might believe that taking breaks is unproductive, but the truth is that your productivity can be given a huge boost when you take breaks more often. Giving yourself some time to unwind helps you recharge. As a result, you end up doing more in less time. This is what effectiveness and efficiency are all about. They both account for your productivity.

The Importance of Decluttering Your Mind

Decluttering the physical space around you will help you create more space for more important things. In addition, such tidiness will also have an impact on your mind since everything will be organized and you will know where everything is. There are few things reminding you that they need to be arranged. Likewise, decluttering your mind also has its benefits.

A Decrease in Stress and Anxiety

Clutter will stress you out. Feeling like your mind is messy may make you feel tired since there is a lot to do yet so little time. Similarly, mental clutter will also make you feel unconfident. You will rarely be confident about your abilities. Repeatedly, you will notice that you second-guess everything that you do. All this is happening because your mind can't think straight. There is a lot that it is focusing on and therefore, finding practical solutions to the little things ahead of you may seem impossible.

By using the recommended strategies discussed herein to clear clutter from your mind, you can be more equipped to lower your stress and anxiety levels. Your mind will feel more liberated. The new space that you have created will give your mind the energy it needs to think and make smart decisions. As a result, you will feel more confident about yourself and the decisions that you make.

An Improvement in Your Productivity

Clutter can prevent your mind from achieving the focus it needs to handle the priorities that you have set for yourself. For instance, instead of waking up early and working on an important project, you might find yourself paying too much attention to the emotional burden that is weighing you down. Frankly, this thwarts your level of productivity. You are unlikely to use your time wisely, which affects your productivity.

Eliminating unwanted thoughts and emotions will help you focus more on what is important. You will find it easier to set priorities and work towards them. You will wake up feeling motivated and goal-oriented. In the short run, you will notice an improvement in your efficiency. Over time, you will realize that you're more effective than ever before since there is more that you can do in less time.

Enhanced Emotional Intelligence

There are numerous situations in which we allow our emotions to affect how we perceive things in life. One minute you love someone and the next minute you think that they are the worst and you regret ever meeting them. In addition, these emotions cloud our judgment and we end up making conclusions that are not valid. In most cases, this occurs when there is a lot on our minds that we have to handle. The result is that we fail to deal with these emotions in an effective manner.

Decluttering your mind requires that you get rid of negative thoughts that would lead to negative emotions. As a result, decluttering more often implies that you will master how to deal with negative feelings. You are less likely to allow negative feelings to weigh you down. This is because you understand that they are just emotions and letting them go is the best course of action you can take.

You can transform your life by choosing to declutter your mind. You will end up making better decisions that lead your life in the right direction. However, it is important to note that the decluttering process will only be successful if you know where the clutter is coming from. To start, you can evaluate yourself and find out why there is so much clutter in your mind. Is it because you overcommit yourself? Is it because you are overwhelmed with the challenges that you have to handle? Is it caused by your fear of making mistakes? Knowing the reasons for clutter ensures that you can control clutter in the long haul. In addition, the digital age that we're living in should not be an excuse to fill your mind with unwanted information. Feed your mind with quality information that drives you to achieve your goals. Curb your information intake and free yourself from clutter.

Chapter 3.   Challenging your Thoughts

To stop overthinking, you need to first retrain your brain. Fortunately, there are many exercises and activities that you can use to reshape the way you think.

Now that you know a little about overthinking, and you also know when you are on the verge of dropping into that deep whirlpool of infinite negative emotions, you can start getting rid of it entirely, and you can start by challenging your thoughts before they run out of control.

Before You Begin

Here are some of the things that you need to know before you start challenging your negative thoughts so you will not get too surprised and overwhelmed with everything that is happening.

1. You need to know that challenging your thoughts might feel unnatural, sometimes even forced at first. But with a bit of practice, it will start to feel natural and believable.

2. To build up your confidence for thought challenging, you should practice them on thoughts that are not as upsetting and provides a bit more flexibility. It is also a good idea to practice this technique when you are still feeling a bit neutral and not too overwhelmed by your thoughts. Trying to practice thought challenging after a particularly rough and problematic day would be asking too much from yourself.

3. The first couple of times you try thought challenging it would be best if you jot down your responses. Often, when beginners try doing it in their heads, they end up with their thoughts going around in circles, which makes their thoughts all the more intense, and might cause them to spiral into overthinking.

4. Another benefit of taking down notes is that if a similar thought pops up in the future, you can refer to your notes and find out how you reacted to it.

5. You can practice with a family member or a friend whom you know will not judge you. Practicing with another person might help you by shedding light on the blind spots of your thinking, or they can offer you different viewpoints that you might find useful.

6. When you are first practicing thought challenging, you should focus on a single thought instead of a series of them this early in the game. For instance, instead of thinking "It's pretty obvious that my bosses thought I messed up the project" you should break down your thoughts into smaller, simpler sentences, and then challenge these thoughts one by one. You will only be confusing yourself if you start challenging a pile of thoughts at the same time.

7. Do something that will distract yourself once you finish working through a couple of thought challenging questions. This will give you some time for your mind to settle down.

Now that you know what you should expect, here are some of the most popular thought challenging exercise that you can try now.

Step Back and Assess the Situation

Here's a scenario that you might have experienced: you feel as if your boss is constantly and intentionally ignoring you. You think that the reason why your boss did not greet you this morning is because you somehow messed up something and that he is contemplating on firing you very soon. Usually, this kind of thoughts will cause your mind to overthink and cause you to lose sleep, thus causing you to not be as efficient at work, which therefore leads to you getting fired; in short, overthinking problems turns them into self-fulfilling prophecies.

On the other hand, if you just step back and analyze your thoughts before your overactive brain blows it way out of proportion, you can control it better. In the case mentioned above, remind yourself that your boss rarely greets anyone at all, and whatever screw up you might have made during the past couple of days is not grounds for your termination. Next, think about what you could do in order to not get fired, like increasing your productivity, or maybe learn a new skill that can help you do your job better.

In just a couple of minutes, you have derailed your train of negative thought before it even gets a chance to gain momentum.

Write Them All Down

Another way to challenge your negative thoughts before they trigger you to overthink is to write them all down on a piece of paper. When you write down the things that are bothering you, it gives them a somewhat tangible form, which actually helps you reanalyze them in a more rational manner. If you want to take this to the next level, you can start making a thought journal.

What is a thought journal/diary?

A thought diary is different from the traditional form of journaling, it has a structure that you have to follow to make analyzing your thoughts much easier. For instance, in a thought diary, you do not start an entry with a "Dear Diary" or any form of it, the entries look more like a ledger if anything.

You make a thought diary by making a couple of columns on the page and then you title them as follows:

Antecedent – These are the things that triggered you during the day.

Beliefs – These are your thoughts about the things that you listed in the first column.

Consequences – These are the things that happened because of your thoughts.

This is why a thought journal is called an ABC journal.

Here is an example on how you write an entry in your thought journal. You suddenly start worrying because you have an upcoming bill that you have to pay, this is your consequence. On the second column, you write that you were worried because you might not be able to make your due date. On the trigger section, you could write that you were watching the evening news when you suddenly remembered that you needed to pay.

After some time of writing in your thoughts journal, you might start noticing that the triggers are usually not related to the thoughts that made you worry. Thoughts just occur, and the triggers that caused them to surface might be related to them at all; thoughts are fickle in that way.

In the consequences column, you then might write down something like, "I took an aspirin to get rid of the headache that I felt was coming."

Every Sunday evening you could review your entries and then think of the things that you could have done better. For instance, for the entry above, instead of taking an aspirin, you could have just walked around the park to clear your mind, or at the very least you could have eaten an apple or something just so your headache will not get any worse. Or you could call your utility company and inform them that you might be a little late on the payment, but you will be paying, and ask if it is possible for them to waive the late fees. Your thought diary will help you make sense of your muddled thoughts by laying them out on paper for you to easily analyze. This tool can help you understand your less-than-ideal coping skills and why you end up making choices that lead to consequences that are not really best for you. With the help of a thought journal you can change your future consequences by restating and reanalyzing your past thoughts and making the necessary adjustments.

Benefits of a thought diary

Writing in a thought journal/diary helps you identify the things that trigger you into overthinking. When you write down your thoughts, you will easily see if they are actually legitimate concerns, or if they are just irrational. Thought journals help you recall how you behaved during the time you were triggered into overthinking, and in time you will start to notice the patterns in the way you think.

When you recognize your existing thought patterns, it will be possible for you to change not only your behavior, but also your thoughts. When you notice evil thoughts start to creep in, you can practice mindfulness (more on this later) and just observe and acknowledge them so they will go away. You actually do not need to behave according to your thoughts, you can actually ignore them and just continue living your own life. It is much better to write down "I ignored the thought of..." instead of "I went to the pub and drank a few pints to make myself forget", and if you notice that you are doing basically the same thing almost every day then your thought diary is actually working.

Make a habit of writing a thought journal

It is highly advisable that you make a habit out of writing down your thoughts using the format mentioned above. You can use a small notebook, a stack of papers, anything that you can write on and keep confidential. No one else aside from you and your therapist (if you are seeing one) must know about the existence of this journal; no one else should have access to your inner thoughts.

If you do not want to use the traditional method, you can also use your smartphone or laptop to create a secret document. Gradually over time, you will start noticing when you are starting to spiral into overthinking and then stop yourself from going any further.

Negative emotions, like those that shatter your confidence to pieces, can usually lead to clinical depression, makes you feel irrationally lonely, hopeless, and they will break you apart from the inside. Writing helps you get rid of your self-destructive thoughts. It is an art that can help you share your innermost feelings and your deepest thoughts.

Writing down your feelings onto paper is a way for you to freely express your views and opinions on the things that happened during the day, and what effect they had on your life. You are not just writing words on paper, you are effectively eliminating all these negative thoughts from your mind, and with them goes all that negativity that came with them.

Get a Hobby

Have you always wanted to learn to play the piano, the guitar, ukulele, or any other kind of musical instrument, why not try learning today? Do you want to get good at drawing, calligraphy, or painting? Attend classes or watch online video tutorials. You can also play your favorite video games for an hour or so. Having a hobby not only gives you a creative outlet, they also provide you with a way to create something with your hands, it also allows you to think individually, and most importantly, hobbies provide you with an escape from your negative thoughts.

Whenever you feel as if your thoughts are starting to overwhelming you, whip out your hobby kit, and immerse yourself in the activity. Lose yourself in the skills, coordination, concentration, and repetition that your hobby requires you to do. Focus your mind on the comfort or challenge brought about by your chosen hobby, and allow it to chase away all of the worries that used to trigger your overthinking.

Meditate Your Worries Away

Meditation can actually help you focus your mind away from the things that are troubling you. In fact, guided meditation can help you reset your mind, thus leaving you unburdened, and refreshed; ready for all the challenges that may come your way.

Meditation is different from mindfulness; the latter is a spur of the moment technique that you can use anywhere and anytime. Meditation, in the purest sense, should be practiced in a calm, silent, and relaxing environment as much as possible.

Here are a couple of meditation techniques. Give them all a try and choose the one that you vibe the most with.

1. Focused breathing

Breathing is one of the body's involuntary actions, meaning you do not really need to command your body to breath, it just happens. However, you can turn your breathing into a form of meditation just by taking notice of every breath that you take.

In focused breathing meditation, you take long, slow, deep breaths; breaths so deep that you fill your abdomen with air as well. To practice this form of meditation, you disengage your mind from all thoughts, and focus all your attention on your breathing. This is especially helpful for when you start noticing that your thoughts are starting to go out of your control.

However, this technique might not be appropriate for those who have respiratory ailments, like asthma and some heart ailments.

2. Guided Meditation

This technique requires you to come up with soothing scenery, places, or experiences that might help you relax better. If you have difficulty thinking up scenes for your guided meditation sessions, you can use any one of the many free apps available online.

Guided imagery is great because you just need to follow the instructions of the smooth voiced instructor and you will be alright. This technique is best for those who suffer from chronic intrusive thoughts.

3. Mindfulness Meditation

As mentioned earlier, this is different from actual meditation. This practice require only that you are sitting comfortably, and then focusing on the present without drifting towards your troubling thoughts of the past and the future. This form is presently enjoying quite a surge of popularity mainly because it can help people who are struggling with anxiety, chronic pain, and depression.

4. Yoga, Tai Chi, or Qui Gong

These three ancient arts might not seem similar, however, they all combine rhythmic breathing with different postures and body movements. The fact that you have to focus on your breathing while engaged in different poses make these activities effective at distracting your mind away from your negative thoughts. In addition, these exercises can also help you gain more flexibility, balance, and core strength. However, if you have a debilitating or painful condition that prevents you from doing anything remotely physical, then these activities might not be right for you. However, you can still ask your physician if you can practice these exercises, he might recommend a good physical therapist or gym that can actually help you. Now, if your doctor believes that it is a bad idea for you to do these exercises, heed his words and look elsewhere for a solution.

5. Repetitive Prayers/Chants

This technique is best for those who have relatively short attention spans, so much so that they have trouble focusing on their breath. For this technique, you recite a short prayer, or even a phrase or two from a prayer while focusing on your breath. This method might be more appealing to you if you are religious or if you are a particularly spiritual person.

If you are not religious, or you do not subscribe to any religion, you can do this by replacing the prayers/chants with positive affirmations or lines from your favorite poem.

Psychological experts advise not just choosing one technique out of the list mentioned above. It is much better to try as many of them as you can and then stick to the one/s that you find effective. It is also recommended that you practice these techniques for at least 20 minutes a day for best results, although even just a couple of minutes of practice can help. However, the longer and more often you practice these techniques, the greater the benefits and stress reduction.

Chapter 4.   Anxiety and Its Causes

In order to treat your anxiety, you need to know where it is coming from. Many people describe it as feeling random. It might seem this way because the onset can seem to be out of nowhere. Overthinking causes and contributes to anxiety. They have a relationship to where they both feed off of one another. If you have anxiety, you have a predisposition to overthinking, meanwhile overthinking will increase your levels of anxiety.

There is a reason people who suffer from anxiety disorder are especially prone to overthinking. This is because their mind has become trained to think in worst-case scenarios. For example, they might be driving, and if they feel the bumps that sometimes happen when you're out on the road, and their mind goes to the idea that they hit something. Let me reassure you of something. You would not think you might have hit something or someone. The impact would be like no other. Not everything can be prevented because things happen sometimes, but as long as you are looking at the road ahead of you and do not have any chemicals in your system that could impede your cognitive function, it is unlikely that you are going to get into any serious accident.

Most of the time, it is not random when a person develops anxiety. Sometimes it comes as a delayed reaction of sorts. You might not feel the effects of it while you're going through a stressful situation because your mind is primarily focused on getting through the situation. After the fact, you go through the psychological effects of your situation because you have time to think about it. This is a common thing that happens to people during stressful situations. We stuff our feelings about it because we want to focus on thinking pragmatically and getting ourselves into a better place.

There have been findings that there are certain chemicals in our brain that can cause mood and emotional disorders when off-kilter. However, there also tends to be an environmental component. There are things that can happen to a person that makes them more likely to have difficulty handling stress. That lies where anxiety becomes a disorder. At a certain level, it is natural. When it passes that point and becomes a hindrance in a person's life, it has become a disorder.

Here's essentially how it works. You have an assignment that is due in two weeks. A healthy level of anxiety will make you think, "okay, I need to do this much work in this amount of time. If I want to make the deadline and put out good work, I can't wait around until the last minute. I need to do this much work every day to reach my goals." When it gets to be about the middle of the day, and you haven't done it yet, you start to feel a little uneasy and remind yourself that you need to get going. It's like a person inside you giving you a nudge to get started on your responsibilities because they want to see you succeed. When an anxiety disorder takes over, you will be overcome with fear when you see the requirements and the deadline. You might think, "there's no way I can handle all of this. How will I come up with that much material in such a short amount of time?" Every time you begin to work on it, the blank page intimidates you, and you decide you'd rather spend your time doing something that does not cause you so much stress. Just the thought of working on it makes your heart rate go up. You tell yourself, "I can't handle this today, I'm going to work on it tomorrow when I'm stronger." Then tomorrow comes, and you use the same excuse to put it off.

Any number of things can cause an anxiety disorder. Everyone has times in their lives when their anxiety is at a heightened level. Major life events, such as illness in the family or the loss of a relationship, come with stress naturally. Even good things like getting a new job can cause anxiety.

One of the biggest reasons endings and new beginnings cause anxiety is because then the question becomes, "What comes next?" People have a natural fear of the unknown. Thinking about the new job, you might be confused because you don't know why you aren't jumping for joy. This might be your first job out of school, or it might be a major upgrade from your last one. The working conditions are better, the pay is higher, and your benefits are greater. However, you don't know exactly how this job is going to be. You might have read what will be expected of you in your new role, but that isn't the same as actually being in the job and going through the motions. You haven't met your coworkers yet, and you have only met your boss very briefly. You might have had to move for this job, so that means you're in a whole new environment. You're in a new neighborhood with people you've never met before, and you will have to find where everything is. You're hoping you don't get lost on your first day at work. Is it now becoming more understandable why you'd be nervous about starting a new job?

Sometimes anxiety disorders are born from trauma. When you think of trauma, you probably think of horrible assaults and natural disasters. While these would definitely be a source of anxiety, don't write off your experiences as not being enough to be trauma. If you had a parent who had a short temper and yelled often, and these temper tantrums didn't take much to provoke, it's easy to see where that would leave you with anxiety. You would be unsure of your social interactions. You would interpret everything people do that seems off as a sign that they are about to become angry because you had been exposed to so much anger.

Thinking about the past can bring on anxiety. It can influence your future. Say you did poorly on your most recent exam. If you spend all of your time beating yourself up about it, you will actually be lowering your motivation to do better next time rather than increasing it. Every time you try to study for the next exam, your mind will go back to the last grade, which will distract you from learning new information. Your morale will be low, and that will decrease your self-confidence. People who do not feel good about themselves will not put in their maximum efforts in what they do because they do not feel that they will do well anyways.

There is no undoing the past. Whether your test score was poor because you didn't study as much as you should have, or you studied the wrong material or didn't get enough sleep, or anything else that could've contributed to the failing grade, you can't go back in time and study properly for your previous exam. That is done. Acknowledging what you did wrong in the past should be an aid in doing better in the future, not an instrument to punish yourself.

The fact that you cannot change the past might be discouraging, but try thinking about it in a different way. If we could go back in time and change what we have done, which we can't, we would never be able to start a new beginning because we would be so consumed with fixing what has already happened. Then, what would be the point of improving as a person? You wouldn't have to because you could just turn back time and act differently, which might change the future in ways you wouldn't expect or want.

The permanent state of the past lifts a burden for everyone it places on us. The only thing we need to worry about is the present and how it will affect the future. Let's say you failed that exam because you spent a little too much time playing video games and too little time studying for it. You know what went wrong. Use the errors of the past in that way only. Use them for finding out how you got the undesired outcome so you can prevent getting a similar one later on. This doesn't mean you have a serious problem with gaming or that you need to give it up altogether. It means you need to find a way to incorporate it into your life so that it doesn't impede other aspects of it. Schedule the time you are going to fit into your day that is reserved for gaming and do not let it go past that. Make sure you have done everything you need to do before you start to do the things you want to.

Make a checklist for yourself about what tasks you need to complete before the end of the day. When you find out what material will be on your next exam, begin setting aside a few hours per day to study. If you have homework, get it done before you log into your game accounts. It can be tempting to start indulging in your hobbies when you get home, but there are a few problems with this. If you do wind up getting to your homework or whatever other things you need to do, you will probably wind up putting it off until it's nearly midnight. Once you get it done, it will probably be early in the morning, and then it will take you a little while after that to get to sleep. You will wake up the next morning feeling tired and groggy, and the work you did last night will have been done with a tired mind. Another possibility is that it will be nearly midnight and you'll decide you're too tired to do it tonight, and therefore put it off until tomorrow morning. This causes you to spend the next morning completing your assignment in a blur, and that is if you have enough time to do so and don't have to hand in a paper that has objectives that go uncompleted.

You will actually have more time to indulge in your hobbies and have more fun doing them if you do what you need to do first. If you have the fact that you have some homework you need to do while you are playing your games, the whole experience will be a stressful one because the thought is always hanging over your head- "When am I going to put away the game and get to my assignments? I'll do it right after this match. No, I'm just going to do one more, and then I'll get to it. Okay, I've got 4 hours to it, I've got plenty of time. I still have three hours. I'll play for just a little bit longer. Oh no! I only have half an hour left! Where did the time go? I have to start now! Please let me finish on time."

The very stress of the situation will cause you to stay in your gaming and not tackle your homework. You think, "it's too stressful to think about doing that assignment, and this is relaxing me, so I'm going to keep doing it." However, you're not really relaxed. You can't be because you have a thought looming over you and nagging you in the back of your mind. The stress builds underneath because you know that no amount of doing nothing is going to make that assignment go away. In fact, the more time that passes, the more real it gets because you know you can only put it off for so long.

Keeping a schedule and sticking with it will take a very heavy weight off of your mind. It will also give you a sense of accomplishment. As you check things off your to-do list because you have completed them will make you feel more confident. When the list has been completed, you will feel good about yourself when you go to bed because you will know you have done everything you need to do.

Young adults often feel a great deal of anxiety due to social expectations. The way society is now; you are viewed as a child who needs to ask permission to do anything until you turn 18. At this point, you are seen as an adult in the eyes of the law, and now you are being expected to find out what you are going to do with your life. You've needed to go to your teacher for a bathroom pass, and now you're being bombarded with questions about what you are going to do in the way of a career. You go off to college, where you find out that you need to occupy yourself, and you also are solely responsible for making sure you have all your assignments done on time and know everything you will need to do in the near future. That has not been the case in the past. This is overwhelming. However, at least during your college years, there is a resemblance to your old life. Afterward is when many people find themselves feeling lost.

There is a growing problem following college graduation where people go through a period of not knowing what to do. They are struggling to find a job that is related to the field they got their degree in, or any job at all. This inspires depression, as well as anxiety. In fact, that is why it has earned the name "the post-graduation depression." Graduates feel depressed because they have nothing to do and as a result of the guilt they feel for not having "launched" yet. It is also a time of great fear. You are wondering if you are ever going to be able to start your life. You may be feeling pressure from your parents to get your career started because they are looking at your situation using their own memory of when they were your age, not realizing the economy and society have changed since then, and it is much more difficult for a person to get started with their life now.

First, go to sleep at a reasonable time and get up early in the morning. When you are nervous about your future, you can find yourself in a habit where you fall asleep at a very late hour and then sleep until sometime in the afternoon. This is an avoidance tactic because then you can say, "Well, it's too late to go job hunting now, the day is almost over." You can' avoid your life. It will happen with or without you in the driver's seat. Set a certain number of job applications per day. Eventually, someone will say yes.

Also, think about exploring alternative career paths. For example, if you excel in writing, or just have an interest in it, you might want to consider freelance writing. You might choose to supplement your income with it, and for some people, it is their full-time career. It might seem impossible to start, but once you get that first client, you've gotten a foot in. Then you will find your second client. Most companies need a writer. You can be a blogger, a technical writer, a fictional writer, anything you can possibly think of; there is a niche for it in the writing business.

While you are searching for your career, do not beat yourself up about where you are compared to everyone else. You are where you are, and that is fine. Before you get started, use the time you have in between for self-discovery. Once you get into the workforce, it will be a consistent thing, so use this time in between for self-betterment. Figure out who you are, and not just in terms of finding your career. In fact, when you have done some self-reflection, it might be easier to find what you want to do with your life. Feel free to try a few career paths before you settle on one. Think long and hard about whether this is something you could see yourself doing long-term. Do not beat yourself up about what you haven't done. That won't get you anywhere. Celebrate what you have done, and know that you are going to do more in the future.

Holding wasted time against you is pointless and will only lead to wasting more time. It is a road to nowhere. Making yourself suffer over a mistake does not undo it. Treat yourself the way you would a close friend who had made a mistake. You would not remind them over and over of the things they did wrong, and if someone tried to do that, you would probably stand up for them and tell that person they couldn't talk to your friend that way. Be a friend to yourself. Stand up for yourself and tell that voice in your mind it doesn't get to insult you, and you take it lying down. Let it know you will make up your own mind about yourself and that your self-esteem will have nothing to do with any unkind remarks it makes.

The most important thing to remember is that once you have improved your behavior, you need to congratulate yourself on that instead of focusing on the errors of the past. Not only will you not undo those mistakes, but you will prevent yourself from achieving future successes. Absolve yourself of the past so your focus can be on the future.

Chapter 5.   Dealing with procrastination

Is there really a connection between overthinking and procrastination? Why yes, there is, and it is actually more harmful than your garden-variety procrastination. Procrastination as a result of overthinking is called "analysis paralysis", this means you have so many thoughts running through your mind at once that you cannot pick just one. You have to pick apart every option that you have until you are satisfied, which rarely is the case (overthinkers usually never come to a conclusive choice).

This is one of the ugliest facets of overthinking that does not really get too much attention, mainly because people do not equate procrastination with overthinking and anxiety; they believe that procrastination is just a byproduct of laziness, and that is sadly not the case.

What is Analysis Paralysis?

Before going deeper into this harmful habit, consider the ancient fable about the Fox and the Cat. The Fox and the Cat were talking in the forest, the Fox said "I can never be caught by the hunters because I have hundreds of ideas on how I can easily escape them!" The cat, who is a bit jealous, said "You are so lucky, I only know one way to escape capture." Upon hearing this, the fox just gloated and chided the cat for not being as smart as he is.

Suddenly, in the distance, the pair heard the bawling of a group of hunting hounds. The cat quickly clambered up the tallest tree he could find so he can escape. The fox, on the other hand, just stood there contemplating which of his hundred or so escape ideas he should use today; he got so engrossed in his thoughts that the hunters' hounds caught up to him and captured the bewildered Fox. Originally, the lesson of the story is to not let your hubris cloud your judgment, but it can also be used as a classic example of the dangers of Analysis Paralysis.

Analysis paralysis, as the name suggests, is the state of over-analyzing (or overthinking) situations so much that a clear decision or action is not taken, which leads to the paralysis of the outcome.

When a person is experiencing analysis paralysis, he gets so engrossed into the analyzing and evaluating of data need to make a correct decision, just like the fox in the fable, you will never reach the right choice, you will just be stuck there with your mouth agape and unable to take any form of action.

Analysis paralysis happens when one's fear of what could potentially go wrong is stronger than the actual realistic potential for success. This imbalance results in the suppression of a person's decision-making in an effort to preserve and try out other existing options. This surplus of available options can make the situation more overwhelming than it actually is and thus causing a sort of mental paralysis, which renders the person unable to make up his mind.

Analysis paralysis becomes an even bigger problem when a decision is direly needed in critical situations, but the person in charge cannot decide fast enough, thus resulting in an even bigger problem than before if only a fast decision was made.

Casual Analysis Paralysis

There are different forms of analysis paralysis, but there are two main distinctions: personal and conversational analysis paralysis.

Personal Analysis

Casual analysis paralysis can happen when you are trying to make a personal decision, but you cannot because you are overanalyzing the situation that you are currently facing. This happens when the sheer volume of information that you have to process starts to become too overbearing. You get so burdened by the amount of things in your head that you cannot, for the life of you, make a rational decision.

There are some cases wherein the decision-maker could successfully analyze every possible outcome, and even write them all down, but then inexplicably trash all of them because he did not like how he analyzed them. Not only is this a waste of mental and physical energy, it is also a waste of your time, which is not a good look when this often happens to you while you are at work.

Conversational Analysis

Analysis paralysis can happen at any time during any typical conversation, however, conversational analysis paralysis usually happens when discussing intellectual and heavy topics. During the course of an intellectual discussion, a person might over-analyze a specific issue, up to the point that the original subject of the conversation is lost. This usually happens because complex intellectual subjects are interconnected with other intellectual issues, and the pursuit of these other branches of discussion somehow makes logical sense to the participants. However, this actually does not make much sense because it muddles the conversation, and the topic of discussion strays so far from the original.

How Overthinking is Holding You Back

Delaying action while over-analyzing available information does not help with productivity. A 2010 survey done by LexisNexis (a legal research company) showed that employees spend more than half of their workday just receiving and analyzing information rather than doing their jobs. However, that is just what people see on the surface. Studies in the field of psychology and neuroscience showed that analysis paralysis takes a bigger toll on you than just wasting your time.

Here are some of the ways that analysis paralysis is holding you back:

1. Analysis paralysis negatively affects your performance on mentally-demanding tasks

Your working memory allows you to focus only on the information that you need to finish your tasks. Unfortunately, you only have a limited supply of working memory per day. Once you have used up all of your available working memory you cannot fit any more information in your brain.

Research showed that high-stress situations can lead to decreased performance when doing mentally-demanding tasks, these are the tasks that where you rely heavily on your working memory to finish. In addition, if there are more participants who want to perform well on a task, the more their performance suffers. Researchers believe that anxiety and stress produces distracting thoughts that take up a lot of your working memory that you could have used to work on your tasks.

2. Analysis paralysis eats at your willpower

A study published by the National Academy of Science looked at the decisions made by parole board judges within a 10-month period. The study found the judges were more likely to grant prisoners parole early in the morning and immediately after eating lunch. They were also more likely to deny parole when the cases are placed on their desk after the end of a particularly long work session. This phenomenon held true over the course of the study, a span that encompassed more than 1,100 cases, regardless of the severity of the crime, which makes it more than just a simple coincidence.

What could have explained these rather surprising, and disturbing discoveries? The judges suffered from what psychology professionals call "decision fatigue". Every decision that people make during the course of the day, like whether to hit the snooze button or not, having fish or chicken for lunch, and other times when you have to choose between several options, they all draw from a limited reserve of willpower. Imagine your willpower as if it was a muscle; the more you use it, the faster you wear it out, which then leaves you mentally exhausted and feeling overwhelmed. This is why dieters have no problem keeping up with their program when it is still early in the day and they are still relatively full after eating a healthy breakfast and lunch, but they are more likely to succumb to the temptation of eating junk food during their afternoon coffee break. During the course of the day the amount of willpower you will have left will dwindle, but it will replenish itself in the morning, only for you to repeat the cycle all over again.

The things that you do without thinking, like brushing your teeth, or putting on your clothes, take little to no willpower at all, so you can still somehow get through the day. However, when you take too long at making a decision, you are quickly depleting what little amount of willpower you have left in your mind.

When you are running low on willpower, your capability to make wise decisions are affected. This means you are more likely to choose to eat unhealthy food, skip exercising, and procrastinate working on your side projects. In short, when you over-analyze your decisions, making more difficult choices even harder in the long run.

3. When you overthink you become less happy

Back in 1956, Herman Simon, an economist, first coined the term "satisficer", which is basically a decision-making style that gives more weight to solutions that are just adequate rather than those that are optimal. Satisficers are people who will only decide once most, if not all of their criteria are met. For instance, they will only stay in a hotel if the in-house restaurant serves the kind of pasta that he wants.

In comparison, "maximizers" want to make the best possible decision. Even when they see something that meets their criteria, they will not make a decision until they have compared it with other possible options. They will waste a lot of their time and energy to find options, regardless if they have little or no significance to the actual task.

Regardless if you are a satisficer or a maximizer, research suggests that your behavior has a huge negative impact on your well-being. These studies found that:

Maximizers are significantly less satisfied, happy, optimistic, has less self-esteem, and has significantly more regrets compared to satisficers.

Maximizers are more prone to suffering from buyer's regret. They cannot help but compare themselves to others and engaging in counterfactual thinking. For instance, they immediately feel sad when they buy an item, they almost immediately think what would have happened if they chose the other item instead. Instead of happiness when they made a purchase, they just feel regret.

Maximizers are more likely to fall into a negative mood once they notice that they did not perform as well as their peers. It's like professional jealousy, but it also spills over to the person's personal life. They constantly compare themselves to people they know, and if they do not perceive themselves to be better than their peers, it will be reason enough to worry oneself into analysis paralysis.

Although analyzing every option available does lead to the absolute best outcome, maximizing will only lead to more stress, anxiety, regret, and you will still not be entirely happy when you do make a decision.

Okay, so now you know how overthinking any decision can and will only make you anxious, kills your productivity, and overall lowers your self-esteem, but what can you do to stop it?

Here are some simple ways that can help you stop over-analyzing your options, avoid getting trapped by analysis paralysis, and just start doing all the things that you are supposed to do:

Structure your day according to the decisions that are most important to you

Not all decisions are equal. For instance, deciding on a brand of toothpaste to buy later is less worthy of your limited supply of willpower compared to, say deciding on whether to agree to the terms of your suppliers or not.

Your ability to make quality decisions wane deteriorate with every choice you make throughout the day, regardless if said decisions are inconsequential or not. This is why you need to schedule your day so that you can minimize the number of decisions that you need to make every day. For instance, divide your workload so that you tackle your most important tasks first thing in the morning, while you still have a lot of willpower to spare. In addition, automate your small, insignificant decisions so that you do not have to waste energy on them. Take Mark Zuckerberg for instance, as head of the biggest social media network in the world, he cannot be bothered to waste energy deciding what clothes he needs to wear, so he wears the same grey t-shirt and jeans combo every day of the week, unless the occasion needs him to change.

Do not even try to tackle big decisions late in the afternoon, you will only drain whatever amount of willpower you have left in your body, and it will only make you feel overwhelmed, cranky, and regretful. If you find yourself getting caught in a downward spiral of overthinking and analysis paralysis, wrestle yourself out of it by doing something that is completely unrelated to your previous task; or better yet, call it a day. Just come back to the task the next morning when your willpower reserves are refilled.

Limit the amount of information you consume

There is a virtually limitless amount of information that you can consult for any sort of problem that you face. For instance, when you are writing a book report, you have an endless number of websites that you can go to for all the important information that you need to know. This is why you need to approach your research with solid intention.

Sherlock Holmes, the greatest literary detective to ever grace the pages of a book, is infamous for only consuming information that he could use in his profession. For instance, Holmes has little to no knowledge about Literature, Philosophy, and Politics, which are subjects that he deems unimportant to his profession. However, his skills in Botany, Human Anatomy, and Geology are variable, he only took various tidbits from the subjects to help him in his cases; for instance, regarding botany, Holmes has an extensive library of knowledge about poisonous plants, especially the ones from the belladonna family.

Holmes knows that the capacity of his brain is very limited so he only stores the information that he needs. Be like Sherlock Holmes, for your workday, only consume information that you will need to finish your tasks; turn off your smartphone, do not open your social media accounts, and do not open your personal email, do those things at the end of the day.

Set a deadline for yourself to make yourself accountable

According to Parkinson's Law, your work will expand to fill the space of time that you set aside for it. For instance, give yourself an hour to finish a task, and you will see that it will take exactly an hour. Give yourself 15 minutes to finish the same task and you could finish it within fifteen minutes. The same holds for decision-making; if you set a deadline for a decision, it will force you to make an efficient decision within that set amount of time.

However, tricking yourself to commit to a self-imposed deadline can be quite hard, but you should find a way that you can hold yourself accountable. One way to do this is to make your deadline as public as possible. Tell a co-worker that you gave yourself a deadline to finish your tasks, or better yet, announce in your social media accounts that you are giving yourself a deadline. The more people who know about your deadline, the better.

4. Stick to your main objective

Identifying your main objective and then sticking to it can help you overcome your tendency to fall into analysis paralysis.

All of your decisions should center around your main objective. If a decision does not affect your main objective in any way, set it aside for later. Only think about the things that you need to do to get closer to your main objective. Because you know your main objective, it helps you make quick and decisive choices because you can immediately assess the options available to you.

Talk with someone else so you can escape your own mind

People are naturally predisposed to overestimate just how unhappy they will be when something bad happens to them, and also overestimate just how happy they will be when things go their way. Studies have shown that complete strangers are actually better at predicting your own satisfaction or dissatisfaction from a decision that you yourself made.

Whenever you are bogged down by a decision that you have to make, just asking another person for his or her opinions about the subject will help you make a decision that you are actually okay with, as compared to making the decision yourself without other people's input.

The next time you find yourself overthinking over a singular important issue, ask a co-worker if you could bother him or her for a minute or so, or you can consult with your supervisor, or if you have one, your mentor. When you present your deliberations to other people, you are actually forcing yourself to synthesize the information in a more clear and concise manner (compared to how muddled and messy the information was when it was still in your mind).

In addition, having someone else validate your ideas, especially if that someone is a person whom you respect, might just be the thing that you need to get over your self-doubt and gain enough confidence to take further action.

Chapter 6.   How to Stop Overthinking

Overthinking is one of the most common mental conditions in the world, and unfortunately, it is also one of the most debilitating. You might think that it is no big deal, everybody gets lost in their thoughts sometimes, right? But when overthinking hits, you, it hits you hard. This is especially troubling if you have trouble with anxiety.

Now, if you have any previous experience in falling into the almost endless spiraling pit of despair that is overthinking, then you know just how horrible it is. Overthinking can prevent you from enjoying the things that you used to love doing, like going to parties, walking in the park, or just meeting with friends. Overthinking can also negatively affect your performance at work, it makes you lose motivation, makes you procrastinate on your tasks, and thus ruining whatever chances of job progression you might have. Overthinking can also ruin your personal relationships; no one wants to be around a person who is always complaining, cranky, and has such a short temper, so you will have very few friends, and they might not be sticking around for much longer.

If the picture painted above seems familiar to you, then you are probably already aware that there is something wrong about you, and that you are already desperate to find a way to fix yourself and start living again. However, it seems like everything you do seems futile, it's as if there is always an insurmountable hurdle in front of you. Overthinking not only leaves you mentally drained, but it also makes you feel exhausted physically. It's like having an energy vampire latched permanently on your neck, and it is constantly feeding on what little mental and physical energy you have.

However, you should not lose hope just yet; there are plenty of ways that you can use to overcome your chronic overthinking problem. But first, you need to start with understanding the core problem; you need to know what overthinking is, and from there, you can start looking for the most viable solutions.

Overthinking Disorder Defined:

Everyone gets sucked into the rabbit hole of obsessive thoughts sometimes, and when it happens occasionally, then it is fine. However, when overthinking starts to consume your life, that is when it becomes a chronic mental problem.

Not everyone is prone to overthink, but some are more likely to suffer from it. For instance, people with a history of struggling with anxiety are almost always dealing with overthinking and its consequences daily. In fact, overthinking is actually one of the triggers that cause anxiety in most people.

Even if you do not have any history of mental health problems, if you consider yourself as a "problem solver" of sorts, then you are prone to overthinking. The thing you consider as your most valuable asset, which is your analytical mind, can become your worst enemy when your overthinking is triggered. Analytical thinkers are the ones that are easily pulled into an endless loop of unproductive and irrational thoughts.

In addition, if you are at a low point in your life where you have unusually high levels of uncertainty, it can trigger your overthinking disorder. If you just experienced a major loss in your life, like you just got fired from your job, your significant other left you, or someone close to you recently died, these events might cause your mind to an uncontrollable spiral of unproductive thoughts.

What are the Symptoms of Overthinking?:

Now that you have an idea of what overthinking is, the next thing that you need to know is the signs of overthinking to look out for. Knowing the symptoms will inform you that you might need to be wary of the status of your mental health, maybe consider getting professional help. You can somehow gauge how deep into overthinking you are by identifying which symptoms have already manifested; if you find that you have signs of being a chronic overthinker, then you should probably consider getting professional help ASAP.

You Have Trouble Getting to Sleep?:

You cannot turn off your thoughts, even when you try; in fact, your thoughts actually start racing even faster when you try to stop them. All of these worries and doubts swirling in your head agitates you and prevents you from getting enough rest.

Overthinkers know the feeling of not getting enough sleep, almost too well actually. Insomnia happens because you have no control over your brain; you cannot shut off the chain of negative thoughts going through your mind at a hundred miles an hour. All of the things that worried you throughout the day come back just when you hit the sack, and you feel so wired that you cannot fall asleep.

If you are having difficulty calming your mind on your own, you can try different relaxing activities before you go to bed. There are plenty of things that might help you ease your mind just enough to let you get some sleep, like meditation, writing on a journal, adult coloring books, drawing, painting, reading a book, or even just having a nice conversation with a loved one. Do anything that can shift your attention away from the negative thoughts long enough for you to get some sleep.

You Start to Self-Medicate?:

Numerous medical researches have discovered that most people suffering from overthinking disorder have turned to use recreational drugs, alcohol, overeating, or other ways to get a grip on their emotions somehow.

Overthinkers feel the need to rely on external stimuli because they believe that their internal resources (aka their minds) are already compromised.

It is never a good idea to turn to try to treat yourself from overthinking. Odds are, you will still be overthinking afterward, and you have to deal with a different problem brought about by your self-medication.

You are Always Tired?:

If you are constantly feeling tired, you need to take action. Fatigue is your body's way of telling you to listen to it because there is something wrong going on; you should not ignore it and just hop from one activity to the next.

Usually, fatigue is caused by physical overexertion and lack of rest. However, overthinking can also cause fatigue and exhaustion. Your mind is like a muscle; if you are constantly burdening it with dozens of heavy, negative thoughts all the time, and not even giving it some time to recover, it will get exhausted and cause you to burn out.

Back when humans were still living off the land, people did not have that many things to worry about, which means they do not have quite as many things to think about as well. In today's modern world, people lead complicated lives that require them to accomplish a lot of things in a short amount of time. In this fast-paced world, the need to slow down every once in a while is crucial for people's well-being. So, whenever you feel fatigued, or better yet, if you feel close to it, slow things down and figure out what your body and your mind need before doing anything else.

You Tend to Overanalyze Everything?:

Overthinkers have one major problem, and that is that they always feel that they need to be in control of everything. They plan out every aspect of their lives, some of them even go as far as planning up to the smallest detail. They feel that doing this is the only way they can feel safe, but it always seems to backfire at them because it is actually impossible to plan for everything that will happen in their lives.

Even so, they still continue to plan out their futures, and they get anxious when unexpected things happen, and they always seem to be unexpected things happening all the time. Overthinkers hate dealing with things that they do not have control over, and they fear the unknown. When unexpected problems do surface, they cause them to sit and mull things over instead of taking immediate action to solve the unexpected problem. Numerous medical studies have shown that overthinking leads to making poor judgment calls, which is why overthinking does not really help.

When you catch yourself just before you start overthinking, try your best to bring your thoughts back to the present by taking deep breaths and thinking happy thoughts. Before your negative thoughts go rampant inside your head, acknowledge them, and think about what they can do for you presently; doing this alone is usually enough to get rid of these negative thoughts because you will discover that their only purpose is to cause you stress.

You are Afraid of Failure?:

You fancy yourself a perfectionist, and you often think about how awful you would feel if you were to fail somehow. This fear of failure can be so strong that it paralyzes you, and it keeps you from learning from your prior mistakes, which often lead to you repeating them.

Overthinkers often cannot accept failure, and they will do everything they can to avoid it. Ironically, they think that the only way to not fail is to do nothing at all. They mistakenly believe that to avoid failure, they should not put themselves in a position to fail at all, which also means they are not in the position to succeed as well.

If this sounds like you, remember that you are more than just your failures; no one could even remember the last time that you screwed up, it's just you. Also, keep in mind that it is impossible to escape failure, and you should never avoid it at all. For failure allows you to grow and evolve.

You are Afraid of What the Future Holds?:

Instead of being excited about the things that you are yet to experience, your anxiety and fear of what could go wrong paralyze you into doing nothing.

If you are afraid of what the future could bring, then your fear keeps you trapped inside your own mind. Research shows that this fear of the future can be so crippling that sufferers tend to turn to drugs and/or alcohol just so they can tune out the negative thoughts that are clamoring inside their heads.

You Don't Trust Your Own Judgment?:

You cannot help yourself from second-guessing all of your decisions, from your outfit, what you will be having for lunch, or even what you will be doing for the day. You are always afraid that you will be making the wrong choices, and you often rely on others to reassure you that you made the right call.

Overthinkers, as mentioned earlier, are natural *perfectionists*; they constantly analyze, re-analyze, and re-analyze again, all situations that they find themselves in. They do not want to put themselves in a position where there is even a slight chance of failure. They do not want to make the wrong choice, so they take their sweet time making up their minds; they do not trust themselves enough to make the right decision for anything. They are

so out of touch from their intuition that all of their decisions come from their brain, and this is not always right as there are times when you just need to follow your gut instinct. Also, if your brain is bogged down from dozens of negative thoughts, it is hard to make a clear decision.

You Suffer from Frequent Tension Headaches?

Tension headaches feel as if there is a thick rubber band wrapped around your temples, and it is slowly getting tighter. Aside from the headache, you might also feel a sharp pain or stiffness in your neck. If you suffer from chronic tension headaches, it is a sign that you are overworking yourself, and you need a rest.

And by rest, it also includes rest from mental activities, like overthinking. Headaches are a sign that your body needs to take a break. This includes your mind. Besides, you might not notice it, but when you overthink, you are actually thinking of the same things over and over again.

Overthinkers usually have negative thought patterns that loop around themselves. To fight this, you need to break this loop by reinforcing positive thoughts. Take deep breaths, and focus your mind on every time your chest rises and falls, being mindful of the present will help you get rid of negative thoughts and the tension headache that came with them.

Stiff Joints and Muscle Pain:

It might sound far-fetched, but overthinking can actually affect your entire body, not just your mind. And once your physical body is affected by your out of control negative thoughts, it will not be long until your emotional well-being gets hit too. Until you address and get rid of the underlying issues that cause you to overthink, the body pains will continue. Overthinking might start in your mind, but its effects will gradually creep into the other parts of your body.

You Cannot Stay In the Present?:

When you overthink, you will find it difficult living in the present moment and actually enjoy your life as it happens. Overthinking causes you to lose focus on the things happening around you, you are so engrossed at thinking about your problems over and over that it seems like you are trapped inside your own mind. If your mind gets bogged down by a ton of unnecessary thoughts, you are removing yourself from the present, and this can and will negatively affect your personal relationships.

You need to open yourself to the world around you; do not let yourself get too wrapped up in negative thoughts. The only thoughts that you should allow inside your mind are those that serve your well-being, ignore, and forget about the ones that bring you down. There is so much beauty in life, and the opportunities for incredible experiences are unlimited. However, you can only appreciate them if you can manage to tune out the idle chatter in your mind and start listening to your heart instead.

Different Causes of Overthinking:

Again, there is nothing wrong about thinking about your problems so you can think of a solution for them, it becomes worrisome when you have a bad habit of twisting narratives around in your head until you can see every angle and side to it. Overthinking is not productive as it just makes you dwell over your problems; you are not looking for a solution for them, and you are only making yourself feel miserable.

To find an effective way to break your overthinking habit, you need to find out what caused it in the first place. Below are some of the more common reasons as to why people tend to overthink their problems rather than actually find a solution for them.

1. Lack of Self-confidence

If you are not self-confident, you tend to doubt every little thing that you say or do. When you hesitate, even a little, about the things that you want to do, you are letting uncertainty and fear creep into your mind, and it will be very difficult to get them out of there. You can never really tell what your decisions will take you; even if you planned every little detail, the outcome will still not be exactly what you hoped for (it could either be better or worse than what you planned). This is why you should learn to take risks and not torture yourself when you did not get the results you wished for.

2. When You Worry Too Much

It is only natural to worry when you encounter new and unfamiliar things and events. However, if you worry too much that you cannot even imagine a positive outcome, then it will trigger you to overthink. This is problematic because worry attracts even more problems, sometimes it creates ones out of thin air, which causes overthinking to go even deeper. Instead of mulling over how things could go wrong, it is better to entertain more positive thoughts, like how much better you would feel if a certain even turns in your favor.

3. When You Overthink to Protect Yourself

Some people believe that they can protect themselves from troubles whenever they overthink, but the truth is that overthinking is a trap that kills your progress. Overthinking and not doing anything to change the status quo might seem good, but stifling your progress is never a good thing at all. Also, when you overthink, you are not really staying in the same position. You are actually undoing whatever amount of progress you achieved thus far.

4. You are unable to "Turn Off" Your Mind

Many overthinkers became that way because they cannot seem to get their minds off their problems no matter how hard they try. People who are sensitive to stress live as if they are constantly wound up tightly; they have somehow forgotten how to relax and change their chain of thoughts. Overthinking happens when a person stresses too much on a single problem, and he could not turn his focus away from it.

5. You are Always Chasing After Perfection

Being a perfectionist is not necessarily a good thing. In fact, one could argue that being a perfectionist is not good at all. Most people who struggle with perfectionism are constantly anxious. They often wake up in the middle of the night, thinking of the things that they could have done better. Being a perfectionist causes overthinking because you are always trying to outdo yourself.

Chapter 7.   How to Stop Overthinking with Mindfulness Meditation

You're familiar with meditation, but what you're going to learn here is how to overcome your excessive thoughts is *mindfulness meditation.* This form of meditation encourages us to remain aware and present by focusing on nothing except awareness of your existing surroundings. Meditation is actually an ancient technique that trains the brain to strengthen its powers of concentration. Sort of like a gym workout, except for your brain this time. Some *archeologists* believe that meditation could be as old as 5,000 years, although scientists only really began studying the brains of those who meditated regularly approximately 60 or so years ago. Still, the fact that this practice has managed to survive for this long means there's something extraordinarily powerful and effective about it.

What researchers have discovered throughout their studies is that meditation changes the structure of your brain, thereby making it a lot more powerful. Long-term meditators have been known to develop almost superhuman-like abilities. For example, their ability to stay calm even in the most stressful situations that would have non-meditators at their wit's end. They could also produce more creative and original ideas, not to mention the better memory they had compared to those who didn't meditate regularly. One *experiment* revealed how meditating monks were able to dry icy wet sheets in cold temperatures by raising and controlling *their body temperature* through the power of meditation.

To understand the way meditation affects us, we need to look at the recent discoveries about how the human brain operates. In the last 10 years alone, what scientists have come to discover is that each time we learn, feel or think something, a new connection appears in the brain. What we repeat the most, like habits, make these connections increase in strength. Simultaneously, the connections that we don't use grow weaker over time until they finally disappear from the mind altogether. This is why habits are automatic and require very little thought to carry them out. For instance, the way you practice brushing your teeth each day makes the task seem a lot more effortless than trying something new like going for a jog in the morning before work. However, if you were to stop brushing your teeth for a few days, surprisingly, it will begin to feel like it requires slightly more effort to execute than it did before.

Some *researchers* have gone so far as to suggest that we don't choose our behavior. Instead, our behavior is programmed by the neural connections in the brain. The brain is like an iceberg, where the tip of the iceberg (the smallest part) represents the conscious mind. Here are all the things we *can choose* consciously, like eating or solving a complicated math problem. The larger part of the iceberg, the one that is submerged and hidden below the surface, is where the unconscious mind resides. The unconscious mind is the one responsible for most of our behaviors since this also happens to be where our thoughts and feelings reside. The unconscious mind, therefore, causes behavior like reacting to arguments in the same way or reacting emotionally more than once, even when we know it's the wrong approach to take. This happens because we're not aware that we're being controlled by the unconscious part of the brain.

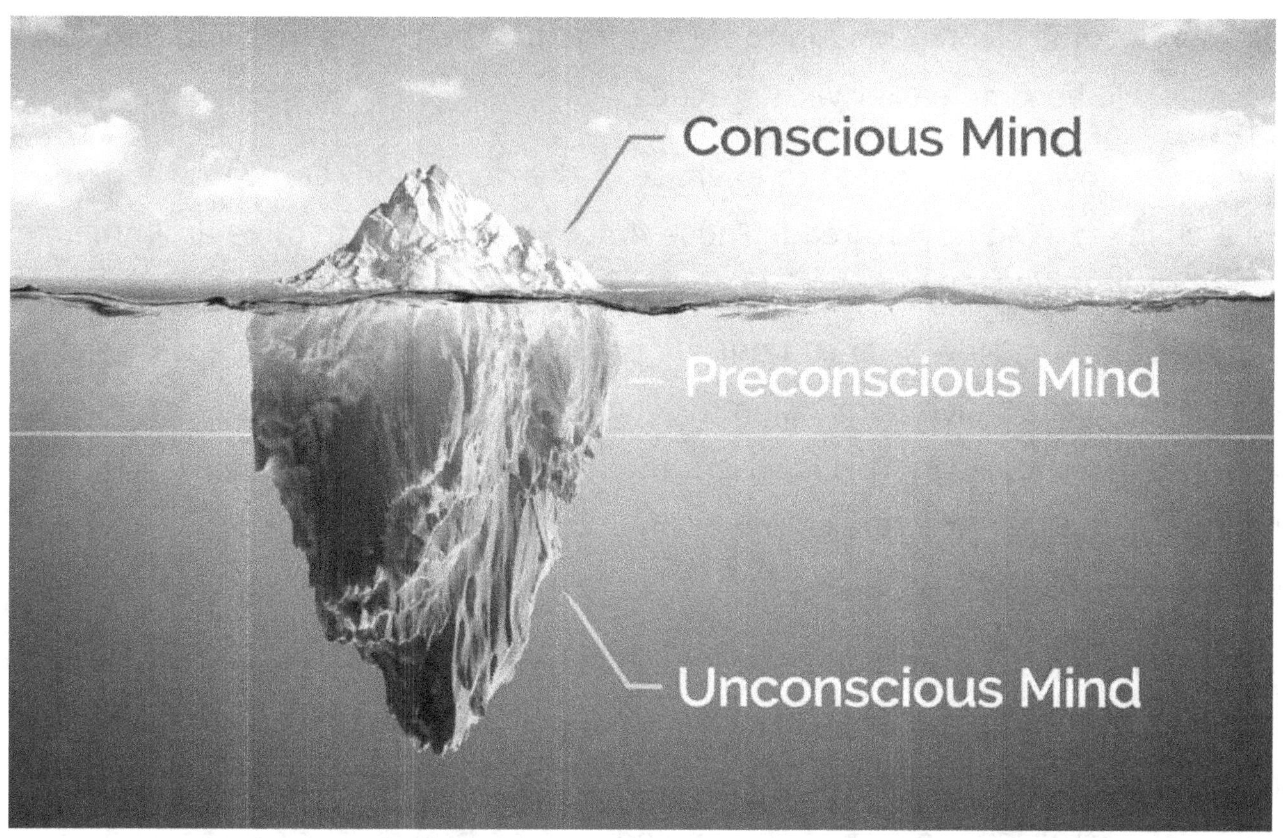

The neural connections in the unconscious part of the mind are strong. This leads to a lot of people to believe that they "cannot change" the way they react or act in certain situations. This automatic response is what we call *personality,* but in actual fact, they are the unconscious mind, emotions, and habits that we keep repeating because it's all we know how to do.

Research has found out that mindfulness meditation can improve focus, memory as well as reduce fixation on negative emotions and lessen impulsive, emotional reactions. *This can be changed.* Everything we know and learn can always be developed through practice. You can train your brain to do what you want it to. To initiate the changes you want to see, you need to first change your brain by creating new connections and then practicing these connections until they become strong enough to be automatic. The things that you find hard to do now will become easier with practice.

Think about how you struggled to exercise in the beginning. Or even when you were a child learning how to read. Those first few attempts felt like an immense struggle back then, but since you kept practicing and persisting, the behavior became automatic. Now, you can quickly breeze through a sentence with ease, and it doesn't take much persuasion for you to put on your workout clothes and start working up a sweat. This is where the meditation practice comes in. It helps us change the structure of the brain by creating new connections in several areas of the brain.

Overthinking leads to continuous stress, and continuous stress leads to mental health issues. Depression and anxiety are very clear examples of what can happen to you if you continue to let your thoughts be the one in control. Meditation decreases the size of the amygdala; the brains fear center, and where all our negative thoughts and emotions come from. Meditation also decreases the levels of cortisol, which leads to an enhanced ability to deal with stressful situations a lot better. During meditation, you'll learn the very crucial skill of learning *how to watch your thoughts and emotions* without reacting to them, which is required for mindfulness. With frequent meditation, there's a possibility of significantly changing your behavior and personality.

How to Meditate

Meditation is one of the simplest forms of mental training you can do. All that is needed is for you to concentrate on your breathing as you allow your thoughts and feelings to come and go. With continuous practice, your skills of concentration, awareness, and attention significantly increase. It does sound easy (and it will be with practice), but in the beginning, you might find that concentrating on your breath is not as easy as it sounds after all.

Where Should I Meditate?

Technically, meditation can be done anywhere you like since it is an exercise for the mind. You could meditate while sitting in a chair or on the floor, even while you're lying down in bed. However, it is recommended that you avoid meditating in bed where possible since you might fall asleep and find it difficult to concentrate.

Sitting down on the floor with your back and spine straight is considered the *optimal* and beneficial way to meditate. This position keeps you wide awake and allows you to sit for a prolonged period while you carry out your concentration session.

What Do I Do When I Meditate?

What should you do with your body while you meditate? Well, the first thing to do is to be aware of the way your feet are positioned. Many regular and seasoned meditators will advise that your feet should be on top of each other. This is not always necessary, though, and you don't have to do it if it doesn't feel comfortable. Beginners might prefer to have their feet crisscrossed on top of each other, sort of like a pretzel while your arms are resting on your thighs. Your hands should be resting on top of each other and form the shape of a cup. If you want to touch your thumbs together while you do this, it's perfectly okay. What matters is that your arms feel relaxed as you keep your back straight and your head level.

Your head should not be tilted upwards or downwards. Relax and look forward naturally. As for your eyes, you have the option of meditating with them open or closed, depending on your preference. Most seasoned meditators prefer to do it with their eyes closed for greater concentration, but again do what feels comfortable and what works for you. If you do choose to meditate with your eyes open, avoid focusing on an object in front of you. Instead, try to look into the distance.

How Long Do I Need to Meditate?

As a beginner, you'll want to set an alarm before you begin your meditation session. When you first start meditating, time tends to feel a lot slower because your body and mind are trying to get used to this new habit. By setting an alarm, you eliminate the constant need to wonder how much time you have left or how long you've been doing it already. Beginners can aim to set about 5-minutes on the clock to start with as you acclimatize yourself to this practice. Once meditation becomes a daily practice and you get used to sitting in this position, you can gradually increase your time blocks, meditating for as long as you want. The recommended time for meditation is approximately 10 to 20 minutes a day.

What Do I Do While I Meditate?

This is the tricky part. There are several forms of meditation that can be carried out. Certain forms of meditation encourage you to focus on your breathing (mindfulness) and loving-kindness, while others may involve chanting a mantra (affirmation). Mindfulness breathing meditation is one of the most commonly taught forms of meditation, and given that you're trying to overcome your overthinking habit, this is the meditation you want to start with.

Mindfulness meditation is easy to learn, and it is considered just as insightful and powerful as any other form. With this form of meditation, you want to start by making sure that you're breathing through your nose. Once you've established a rhythm, focus *all your attention* on your breath and observe the way the air flows in and out of your body. Pay attention to the air flowing in and out of your nostrils; observe the way your breath makes the transition from inhale to exhale. Even pay attention to the little pauses that happen between the moment you inhale and exhale. Don't judge. Don't criticize. Just stay calm and observe; that's all you need to do.

You'll quickly notice that thoughts begin to appear in your mind and will try to distract you from this simple task you're supposed to be concentrating on. If you notice your mind wandering, don't worry. Simply pull your thoughts back toward your breathing and focus on your breath. This is how you start training your mindfulness muscle. Many beginners often find it extremely hard to focus on nothing but the breath, so you're not alone if you feel this is a struggle. If this happens, don't be too hard on yourself or too critical, this is perfectly normal. All you need to do is bring your attention right back to your breathing whenever the mind wanders.

How Often Should I Do It?

Ideally, you want to aim to make mindfulness meditation a daily habit. The more you do it, the easier it will become to focus on nothing but your breath as your mindfulness muscle grows stronger. Meditating every day gives you the best chance of seeing the benefits quickly. You could do it once a day, twice a day, or even three times a day if you have the time. You can do it as many times a day as you like, but what matters most is that you do it EVERY DAY.

How Soon Can I Expect to See the Benefits?

Well, you need to be doing it every day to see the benefits a lot sooner. The length of time you spend meditating daily will also play a factor in how quickly you start experiencing the benefits. Ultimately, it is difficult to fix an exact time frame since the experience is going to differ from one person to the next. Some people happen to be less mindful in general because of the lifestyle they lead and the way they grew up, so they might need more time before they begin seeing any real change. The best thing you can do is to just keep practicing and don't compare your journey to someone else's. It doesn't matter how fast or slow the benefits start to happen. What matters is that if you keep at it, *they will happen.*

Why You Need to Practice Mindfulness

Overthinking is a distraction, and that is just one of the many reasons why you need mindfulness to live in the present. As painful as some of the difficult parts of life is, that's what *living* is, and we need to embrace it wholeheartedly, both good and bad. Mindfulness teaches us that it is still possible to find happiness even in the darkest times. It's not always possible to be mindful 100% of the time, but the following reasons will remind you why you need to make an effort to live mindfully every day:

- *It's the* **Only Real Time** *to Live Properly* - We spend more time than we should when we continue living in our heads worrying about the past or the future. We worry about what we cannot change and what we have no control over. Mindfulness is the only tool that is effective enough to get you to break the habit bit by bit. The past only exists in our memory, and the future is yet to come. This means that the only *real living* that takes place is your present. The here and now.

- *Your Thoughts Are Less Likely to Sweep You Away* - It's impossible to get carried away when you know exactly what's going on with your thoughts, emotions, and feelings. Instead of getting swept away by your excessive thoughts this time, mindfulness will turn you into an observer. Think of your thoughts like a flowing river. You cannot forcefully stop the water from flowing. When you enter the river, you will get swept away, so instead, the better thing to do would be to practice sitting by the river, watching it flow by. By becoming an observer, your thoughts and emotions loosen the hold they have over you. You no longer feel powerless, and like you're drowning. You become calm, composed, and this time you're the one in control. Like the flowing river, the thoughts won't stay forever unless you choose to let them. You're not trying to fight your thoughts, judge it or forcefully change it. You're just there to observe.

- *It Builds Stronger Relationships* - Among the more common worrying thoughts that tend to plague the mind of an overthinker is the anxiety they feel about what others think of them. It's hard to form great connections when you're not really *listening* to what is being said to you. Sure, you're there in front of the speaker, but when you're preoccupied with your thoughts, you're not actively listening, and you miss out on important information that could have been used to strengthen your relationship. Mindfulness can change the type of conversations you have with people by encouraging you to pay attention and be open to their needs. To put aside everything else for those few minutes and pay attention to what is being said to you. Once you start actively listening, conversations seem richer and more meaningful. The other person begins to engage more when they notice you're actively paying attention to them too. It makes them feel like what they have to say matters, and that, in turn, encourages them to be more open and share more of their life with you.

- *It Makes You Aware You Have Everything You Need to Be Happy* - We keep searching for happiness and then getting frustrated when it's seemingly hard to attain. Through mindfulness, however, you realize you already have everything you need to be happy. You couldn't see it because you were too distracted by your thoughts. When you start living in the present, the realization begins to dawn on you that there is no real need to hold on to the things that make you unhappy. You don't need to hold on to grievances about your past or worry about your future. Your eyes begin to open to the fact that perhaps a lot of the problems you have today were created in your mind, and if you break those problems down bit by bit, there might not be anything much to worry about after all. Feeling grateful for the life you have is your biggest defense against negativity. You don't need to rely on external or material things to make you happy when you feel good from within.

- *It Reminds You to Take Care of Yourself* - You can't take care of anyone else if you're not taking care of yourself first. Self-care can be a tough lesson for overthinkers since they tend to cross their boundaries. Their excessive thinking could lead them to push too hard until they eventually get burned out. Mindfulness makes you more aware of your strengths and your boundaries. You're less likely to push yourself too far when you're aware of the way that your mind and your body feel. You begin respecting your body more, and you slowly lose the urge to keep up with society's fast-paced expectations if it is going to make you unhappy doing it. It's perfectly okay to do what makes you happy without having to feel guilty about it.

Chapter 8.   How to Stop overthinking with Positive Self-talk

The practice of positive self-talk is one of the fastest ways to get out of your head. It is the practice of being optimistic and seeing the positive in just about any situation. When you can't see the positive, you are at least aware of the situation enough that it doesn't send you into a tailspin of negative thinking. You are able to see the situation for what it is.

By now, I hope you have been able to identify some of the ways that you are sabotaging your mental health and are now becoming more aware of when it occurs. Now it won't be easy to turn the negative self-talk around, but with some diligence and consistency, it is possible. It requires practice, time, and some grace toward yourself when you slip up.

What is Self-Talk?

Self-talk is the internal chatter that goes on between yourself and your brain. It's this internal chatter that can be both positive and negative, it can be distressing, and this can largely depend on your personality. If you are an optimist, then your inner dialogue will be more positive, which offers some health benefits and a better quality of life. The opposite can be said of being a pessimist, but with diligence and hard work, the negative self-talk can be turned around regardless of your personality and upbringing.

Positive self-talk has many benefits, including enhancing your general well-being, increasing your physical well-being and less stress. Other health benefits can include:

- Increased vitality

- Greater life satisfaction

- Better immune system

- Pain relief

No one really knows why this works and why people with a more positive outlook on life experience these benefits, but research suggests that these people may have the mental skills to be able to cope with stressful situations, which can reduce the harmful effects of stress.

Louise Hay, the well-known author of Heal Your Life and Heal Your Body, put this into practice when she was diagnosed with cervical cancer in 1978. She considered alternative options to surgery and instead decided to put together her own intensive program. Using affirmations, visualizations, nutritional cleansing, and psychotherapy she was able to cure her cancer completely within six months.

How to Practice

It will take time to catch the negative self-talk because it's become so ingrained in you and feels so normal, but it can be changed with practice. Once you start to recognize your patterns, then you can start to address the best practices for you.

Examples:

Negative: I failed, why did I even try? Now I'm embarrassed.

Positive: Wow! I'm proud of myself for trying something new. That was brave of me.

Negative: I've never done this before, why did I even try, I'll be so bad at it.

Positive: This is a great opportunity for me to learn something new.

Mirror talk - this may seem silly and feel awkward at first but talk to yourself in the mirror. Look yourself in the eyes and talk. Tell yourself you love yourself, that you love your hair, your eyes, whatever it is, just start talking positively to yourself about yourself.

Affirmations - write affirmations everywhere around your house. On your door as you leave the house, in kitchen drawers, on your bathroom mirror, in the car, etc. Seeing and reading these affirmations will have a positive effect on your brain and boost your serotonin, which is the 'happy' chemical in our brains because it promotes happiness and well-being.

Positive people - look at who you are surrounding yourself with, whether you believe it or not we feed off the energy of those we associate with, so find people that inspire you, lift you up, and cheer you on.

Gratitude

Given all the ideas listed throughout this book, I felt this one deserves its own heading as I strongly believe it is one of the fastest ways to turn negative self-talk into positive and set yourself up for success.

Gratitude is defined as an overall sense of feeling grateful. An emotion expressing appreciation for what you have.

It can exist as both a temporary feeling and an inherent part of who you are. Gratitude requires a recognition of something occurring that was positive and outside of you. While most of this book has been directed at healing our inner world and that is crucial to sorting through overthinking and our anxiety and depression, we also need to accept that some external forces are necessary to make us happy, but we need to show gratitude for these things.

It is generally seen as a spontaneous feeling, but it is also increasingly becoming a part of a practice to count your blessings and be grateful for what's in front of and around you. Because of this, you can deliberately cultivate a feeling of gratitude.

Gratitude Matters

It is possible to feel grateful for loved ones, colleagues, and life in general. This emotion generates an atmosphere of positivity. You will find that over time, this feeling boost happiness and promotes physical and emotional health, even when struggling with mental health obstacles. It may be a little harder to dig for the gratitude in such instances, but with practice, time and consistency you will find it is your go-to for tough times.

Practicing gratitude curbs the negative words and thoughts, and it shifts your inner attention away from anger, resentment, and jealousy, which minimizes the possibility of spiraling downward into ruminating or catastrophizing the situation.

Gratitude starts with noticing the goodness in your life, which can be hard in this world of materialism and constant comparing to others via social media, but it is possible.

It can start small, just noticing something in your day that you are grateful for, maybe it's your job because that allows you to put food on your table, or your house and having a roof over your head so you are safe, maybe it's your car because the crowding on transit makes you uncomfortable. Whatever it is, be thankful, be grateful and show it, acknowledge it. I keep a journal and write in it every morning and/or evening at least three to five things that I am grateful for that day. It has made such a difference in how I view things and react to things.

Gratitude is by far the biggest tool that has seen me through some dark days. Being able to be grateful for any given situation knowing that it is for my highest good has turned most of my negative self-talk and dark thought spirals around to positive. When I catch myself slipping back into a negative frame of mind, all I have to do is quickly list off a few things I'm grateful for and the negativity melts away.

It wasn't always like this; it took time, practice, and consistency.

Now the real magic in gratitude that I have discovered happens when you are able to start being grateful for the people and issues in your life that challenge you. For example, you've just gone through a horrible divorce and custody battle for your children. You loathe your ex for all that he/she has put you through, but without this person, you wouldn't have your amazing kids. You realize that you are grateful to him/her for giving you such a gift. Now, I realize this may sound a little farfetched and hard to fathom, but I can speak from experience that this does work. I have recently gone through this very thing. While I am not a fan of my ex at all, I am extremely grateful for the gift of my child who wouldn't be in this world without my ex. Believe it or not, shifting to this way of thinking has made the court trips and such a little easier to deal with.

If that seems a little difficult in the beginning, then try this:

- Who has inspired you? Why?

- Keep a gratitude journal - Write big and little joys of daily life or try and identify three to five good things that happened that day.

- Try to imagine what your life would look like if some particular positive even hadn't happened.

Chapter 9.   Developing a Winning Mentality

A winning attitude is something that we develop. It is a result of the right conditioning. The same people who look so uber-confident and enthusiastic can become just the opposite of they develop a negative mentality, and the same is true vice-versa.

If you want to get out of the trap of negative thought processes and develop a winning mentality, you will have to bring some positive changes in your personality.

Given below are some small yet important changes that you must make in your day to day personal life and personality to develop a winning mentality. These changes are not very significant, yet they can leave a very deep impact on your conscious brain and the way it perceives problems. This is a thing which will matter a lot when it comes to having a winning mentality.

Start the Day with Positivity

This is a point we have already discussed in earlier chapters, but it can't be stressed enough. The way we start the day has a very deep impact on the way it will end or at least go for the most part.

If you woke up late and from the very beginning, you are worried that the day is going to be bad, you can be sure that you are correct because you have set the tone for the day. On the other hand, if you wake up smiling and leave your home expecting good things to happen, you will have many pleasant surprises in the day.

This is not some magic. When you are in a pleasant mood, even simple things look good. Have you ever felt the way day feels when you have received some very good news? On the day you are in a bad mood, even the best of the weather would mean nothing to you.

This doesn't end here. Your mood is constantly affecting your psyche. It is shouting loud and high that everything is going wrong. It has already accepted that the day has gone wrong, and it is going to end on a worse note. It would take a miracle to lift up such a mood.

Start your day on a positive note, and try to maintain it as far as possible. It would have a positive impact on your mentality.

Focus on Positivity Daily- Find at Least 4 Positive Things of the Day

At the end of the day, daily try to find at least 4 positive things about the day that has just come to its conclusion. This should be done without exception.

It can be anything that you liked on the whole day. You saw a flower, and it looked beautiful enough to lift your mood, mention it. You met a stranger who smiled at you genuinely, that can be a thing to mention. You helped someone in any way that made you feel food; this can be a thing to mention. It can be anything you liked but there should be at least 4 things that you liked about the day.

If you like, you can even journal then in a dairy or just say them out loud. This simple act can help in changing your perspective about the world. You start looking for positivity around you.

Do Something Positive for Others Daily

This is a simple act of kindness that you may do. It can be a minor act. It doesn't have to be anything major every day. But, you must do one thing at least every day that made any difference to the life of one person. When we do some act of kindness, we not only touch the lives of others, but the selfless act also touches a corner of our self too and lifts our spirit and mood.

It fills you with a sense of happiness and you feel proud of yourself either other people acknowledge it or not. It is a change that can help in infusing positivity in your mind.

Live in the Moment

You must learn to live in the present. You must stop reflecting too much on the past. Live every experience as it comes, and please stop judging things on the basis of your past experiences. This will give you a fresh perspective. Change is a reality and constant truth. The only thing that is constant is change. When we judge things on past experiences, we are coming in the way of this change.

Appreciate Yourself

This is important. You must learn to appreciate the genuine qualities in yourself. You must try to look for strong points in your personality and work on developing them. The more you appreciate yourself for your qualities, the easier it would get to break the negative thinking process.

Appreciating yourself is important if you really want to be successful in your relationships, job, and life in general. The people who are not even good enough in their own eyes can never expect to be good enough for others. If you don't appreciate yourself, you'll keep feeling stressed and insufficient. There will always be a problem with your overall satiety levels.

Find Avenues to Remain Motivated

Remaining motivated is important. You must find all the ways that are there to remain inspired and motivated. From movies to ted-talks, whatever works for you should be used to get the required push. Motivation keeps giving you the boost to continue working with the same force.

Work on Your Body Language

It is important that you work on your body language. From your clothing to the way you conduct yourself, everything in your personality should speak of your confidence and positivity. You must remember that positivity and negativity both are contagious. A positive person can light up the whole room while a negative person can make the people around gloomy. You should pick the type of person you want to be.

Remember that it is more important for you than it is important for others. Your attire, appearance, and conduct all have a deep impact on the way your mind functions.

Appreciate and Be Grateful More Often

Make it a general rule to appreciate others even for minor things that help you or make your life easy. It is another positive change that can help your mentality a lot. When you are saying positive things about others, you are reminding your mind to think in the same way. When you are expressing your gratitude for others, you are being more open, accepting, and acknowledging. This has a very deep impact on your conscious mind.

Look for Positivity Even in Grim Situations

This is a no brainer. You can't lose all hope when things start to go south. A big part of winning mentality is to maintain composure even in grim situations when others are losing hope. It is an art that needs to be developed.

Look for Solutions and Not the Problems

You must look for the problems and not the solutions. This is a statement we often hear. However, as soon as things get out of control, our mind starts looking for escape routes or even better starts exaggerating the problems. We don't contribute anything; on the contrary, we end up making things worse.

All this happens because our mind remains focused on the intensity of the problem and not on the solution. You must remember that thinking about the problem and the amount of damage it can cause can never solve it. You will have to start thinking about the way to resolve it. It is a talent that will need to be cultivated.

Conclusion

Congratulations on making it to the end of the book. It's never easy to admit that you have a problem with stress. It's something that we all experience, and it can also be something that ruins our lives. If you are not careful, then you will start to realize that stress isn't just something that you experience, but it becomes part of who you are. The longer you go without managing stress, the harder it will be to manage these feelings when you need to the most.

Remember that it is all a mental thing at first, but if not treated, it can turn into a physical problem rather quickly. Don't let the physical side of stress take over your body. You are the one in control! Not only will stress make you experience pain in your shoulders, jaw, and other parts of your body, but it will also increase your risk for more serious health conditions, such as stroke or heart attack.

What stresses you out isn't something that is going to stress others out every time either. What calms you won't calm other people. Don't compare yourself, because we all will always have differing perspectives on what is stressful, as well as how to react to our positive and negative emotions. Sometimes you might wish you could be that chill relaxed person, but remember that not everyone is always as calm as they might seem. There's nothing wrong with you if you find that you are stressed in a situation that others are completely fine. It doesn't matter what stresses you out. The most important thing is how you react to this feeling.

Always check in with yourself and ensure that you are doing your best to calm yourself at the root first. Challenge your thoughts and question your beliefs to see where the stress might have started. Just because a thought travels through your mind doesn't mean that it is true. Sometimes, we think of what we were taught to believe first, and the second thought that comes after can be what's most important.

Keep up with research on stress and anxiety as well. There will always be new ways for you to manage your stress. Since we still have yet to completely figure out our brains, there will always be emerging science around what it is that might make our brains operate in the way that they do.

Remember that everything is temporary. Everything is going to be OK in the end. You are the one that is creating stressful thoughts in your head. Sometimes you are just going to have to sit with your discomfort and feel the stress. It will end. Panic attacks will stop, and your stressful thoughts will calm down. Nothing that you experience is going to last forever.

Others say things that might stress you out, but you will always have options for how you react to these stressors. You won't always be able to stop others from causing you harm, and there will be plenty of people that will always know how to get under your skin. Though you are powerless in this, you are entirely in control of the way that you choose to handle these situations. Look for the ways that will help alleviate your stress the best.

You are not alone in the stress that you feel. Though you might feel isolated, crazy, too emotional, and plenty of other negative feelings associated with your stress, remember that this is a common emotion. You are not wrong, broken, bad, or crazy because of the emotions that you are feeling.

The things that you see online always have truth behind them. Don't let social media or inflated news articles cause you to have more stress than you already do. When you see a particularly upsetting news story, always check the sources. Take a break from your phone and really give yourself time to be quiet with your thoughts.

You might feel like you aren't doing well, but there is always going to be someone out there that is jealous or admires you. Everyone thinks that they're doing bad, but most of the time, we're doing a lot better than we'd think. Remind yourself of this in times that you are feeling more inadequate than anything.

Those who are important to you wouldn't judge you for the things that you are hard on yourself for. The ones who matter most are those people that will love you unconditionally. If anyone makes you feel bad about yourself, causing you even more stress than you initially had, remember that they are hurting. The only reason that you would want to bring someone down is because that is the way that you might already be talking to yourself! Others might still judge us, say rude things, and think negative thoughts, but that doesn't have to affect us. You know your own worth, you have your values, and you are in charge of your emotions. This is what matters the most.

You will always remember the most important things at the end of the day. When you are laying in bed alone with your thoughts, this is when you will remember the truth of your life. When everything else is stripped away - work, relationships, money, and so on, that is when your true character is revealed. You are your own person and that is beautiful!

We all have different speeds that we move through our day and in life. What you take slower might be something that others speed through. The things that you get over in a snap might be someone else's long journey. The less you compare yourself to others, the easier it will be to love yourself for who you really are.

Sometimes, you will have to laugh it off. Certain situations might be so stressful that the best thing you can do is just smile and keep pushing forward. If everything feels like it is falling apart around you, just look in the mirror and try and make the biggest grin possible.

When you are really stressed out, you can gently blow on your hands or arms. Give yourself something to fixate on, such as chewing gum or mints. Fill your home with the right kinds of colors and other things that keep you feeling good. Pick the right scents, such as lavender, to help reduce your stress. These things can seem so small, but they can really help to carry your mental health past its limits!

There are so many ways that you can reduce stress, and it is time for you to emphasize this now. It will only get worse as time goes on, so there's no better time to alleviate stress than right now!

www.ingramcontent.com/pod-product-compliance
Lightning Source LLC
Chambersburg PA
CBHW080458030726
47592CB00011B/3160